The Book of Common Prayer

The Book of Common Prayer

A Spiritual Treasure Chest— Selections Annotated & Explained

Annotation by
The Rev. Canon C. K. Robertson

Foreword by
The Most Rev. Katharine Jefferts Schori

Preface by
Archbishop Emeritus Desmond Tutu

Walking Together, Finding the Way ®
SKYLIGHT PATHS®
PUBLISHING
Woodstock, Vermont

The Book of Common Prayer:
A Spiritual Treasure Chest—Selections Annotated & Explained

2013 Quality Paperback Edition, First Printing
Annotation, and introductory material © 2013 by C. K. Robertson
Foreword © 2013 by Katharine Jefferts Schori
Preface © 2013 by Desmond Tutu

Library of Congress Cataloging-in-Publication Data
Available upon request.

10   9   8   7   6   5   4   3   2   1

Manufactured in the United States of America
Cover Art: The title page from the 1552 version of the Book of Common Prayer.
Cover Design: Walter C. Bumford III and Tim Holtz

SkyLight Paths Publishing is creating a place where people of different spiritual traditions come together for challenge and inspiration, a place where we can help each other understand the mystery that lies at the heart of our existence.

SkyLight Paths sees both believers and seekers as a community that increasingly transcends traditional boundaries of religion and denomination—people wanting to learn from each other, *walking together, finding the way.*

SkyLight Paths, "Walking Together, Finding the Way" and colophon are trademarks of LongHill Partners, Inc., registered in the U.S. Patent and Trademark Office.

Walking Together, Finding the Way
Published by SkyLight Paths Publishing
A Division of LongHill Partners, Inc.
Sunset Farm Offices, Route 4, P.O. Box 237
Woodstock, VT 05091
Tel: (802) 457-4000   Fax: (802) 457-4004
www.skylightpaths.com

Contents ☐

Foreword □

The Most Rev. Katharine Jefferts Schori
Presiding Bishop of the Episcopal Church

Episcopalians and Anglicans claim to be related by shared prayer, rather than by a list of beliefs. We are people of *common* prayer, both in the sense of shared prayer and in the sense of prayer that sees the holy in the everyday. Our prayer has particular contextual roots in the early Celtic Christian forms that offered prayers for milking cows and plowing fields, blessings for boat journeys and walking ones, and richly beautiful language that invokes a sense of God's presence in all times and places. Our prayer is common and continual, through the hours of the day and the changes and seasons and chances of this life.

The Book of Common Prayer was originally a way to seek healing among a divided people, and it continues to serve that holy purpose— being used today by people and congregations who are not avowedly Anglican but find the meter and imagery of its prayers to be holy and for-mative. God is working a small reconciliation of the larger body of Christ through these shared prayers. The reader will discover something of the diversity of the Prayer Book tradition, both historically and in today's global Anglican Communion.

Canon Robertson brings a deeply pastoral sense to guiding the reader through the riches of the Episcopal Book of Common Prayer, repeatedly pointing to ways in which it can undergird the spiritual discipline and forma-tion of individuals, families, and communities. This is a resource that invites, encourages, educates, and makes rich connections for the seeker. There is treasure abundant here and deeply fertile possibility for forming a more hon-est, thankful, and joyful spiritual life in one who begins to use it regularly.

The ancient riches here are also new every day of one's life. Structuring time around regular prayer grounds life in relationship with the holy and imbues all of life with a sense of gratitude and hope. Those patterns were honed by monks and nuns through the ages, but they have their ancient roots in Hebrew tradition. Robertson offers a remarkable gift in the intimations that Thomas Cranmer or Queen Elizabeth I wrote or prayed a particular passage—giving an inkling of what leadership or pastoring or simply faithful living and endurance were like in a particular age. It gives a far more expansive view than what we usually receive through the external data of history—wars, convulsions, rebellions, and the like, rather than the private prayers of those who lived and led through them. That becomes a deeply hopeful resource for those who pray today.

Grounding one's life in regular rounds of prayer can connect us with Jesus's own life and ministry and permit us as well to see the "hand of God at work in the world about us."[1] That may be in giving thanks for food to eat, or the blessing prayed over newlyweds, or in encouraging our concern and response toward those in need and God's wider creation.

This is a resource for life—all of life—and Robertson offers a robust and creative invitation to enter, explore, and use the deep wisdom of the Book of Common Prayer in your own life and that of your community. As one of the prayers of this tradition says, "read, mark, learn, and inwardly digest" this rich food, born of relationship with God through the ages, and find your life transformed.

1. Proper 28 from the Collects of the Church Year, *The Book of Common Prayer* (New York: Episcopal Church), 236.

Preface □

The Most Rev. Desmond Tutu
Archbishop Emeritus of Cape Town & Nobel Peace Laureate

It is a wonderful thing to pray. And it is a more wonderful thing to pray together! God loves diversity and God loves unity, and when the two merge, unity in diversity and diversity in unity, then something truly miraculous can occur. This is at the heart of common prayer—different people of all types coming together and embracing God. In this latest volume in the SkyLight Illuminations series on sacred texts, Dr. Robertson makes much of the term "common" prayer. He shows how Anglican Christians have relied on common prayer, not agreement on doctrines or unanimity in ideas, to stay connected to one another.

God made us all different so that we can come to know how we need one another. Archbishop Thomas Cranmer, who oversaw the creation of the first Book of Common Prayer, and all those who have revised it at different times and in different places, understood this simple truth. We need each other. And because all of us are by nature worshipful, when we worship together we are the richer for it. It is little surprise that when some people choose to break away from their sisters and brothers in faith, one of the first things they do is cease to pray together.

I have often said that we realize our human potential only when we truly reach out and accept one another and accept our need for one another. This is why I invited P. W. Botha, the president of South Africa during some of the darkest times of apartheid, to join our side, to join the imprisoned and persecuted, because in God's moral universe we had already won. Common prayer means inviting both our friends and our enemies to join us in worshipping the God who loves not just some of us, but all of us.

I previously contributed a preface for another of Dr. Robertson's books, *A Dangerous Dozen: Twelve Christians Who Threatened the Status Quo but Taught Us to Live Like Jesus* (SkyLight Paths). Those twelve Christians who challenged their respective power structures were very different people in very different contexts, but they all shared not only a passion for God's peace and justice, but also a strong and healthy prayer life. They, and many others like them, went to God in adoration, in contrition, in thanksgiving, and in supplication because they knew that this is where they would find their strength for the challenges that awaited them.

Whether it is Cranmer's 1549 Book of Common Prayer, the Aotearoa/ New Zealand Prayer Book, or my *African Prayer Book*, what we find in these treasure chests are spiritual gems from many different sources which, when put together, form a wonderful unity ... much like the people who make use of them. It matters not if you offer these prayers together with others or alone, for every time you pray with humility and a thankful heart, you are praying in common with all those other humble, thankful children of God.

So enjoy this study of a very special, important text, The Book of Common Prayer. Lose yourself in words both ancient and fresh. Find yourself in relationship with God and with others who share your common needs, hopes, and prayer. And in the end, as the great African bishop and saint Augustine of Hippo promised, "All shall be Amen and Alleluia."

God bless you.

Desmond

Introduction □

So that here you have an order for prayer (as touching the reading of the holy Scripture), much agreeable to the mind and purpose of the old fathers, and a great deal more profitable and commodious, than that which of late was used.

PREFACE TO THE 1549 BOOK OF COMMON PRAYER

It is a book born in the fires of reformation and revolution, and yet it emphasizes continuity and harmony. Its very title points to the goal of "common" prayer—a double entendre, intentional or otherwise—alerting any who would open its pages that this work is for all, whatever one's status or station, be it priest or layperson. And it is a book that is for all together. For centuries, Christians of different traditions and seekers from various backgrounds have found both strength and solace in the pages of The Book of Common Prayer (BCP).

What is it about this book that has made such an impact in the lives of so many? What's so special about The Book of Common Prayer, and perhaps more to the point, how can it prove useful to you on your own spiritual journey?

First composed in 1549, the Prayer Book, alongside Shakespeare's works and the King James Bible, helped shape the English language. Having been revised several times through the years to account for different local contexts, today it is used in one form or another by almost eighty million Anglican Christians throughout the world. Its familiar words and rites for marrying and burying have become part of our culture, often borrowed by other religious traditions and commonplace in Hollywood films and television. Presidents, monarchs, and Nobel laureates; poets, musicians, and comedians; peacemakers and change agents alike are among those who have claimed the Prayer Book and its spiritual treasures for their own.

A Guide to Finding God in the Everyday

As for me, I did not discover the Prayer Book until I was in my twenties. I grew up in a household where my mother was Southern Baptist and my father was Roman Catholic. From my mom I heard, "The Bible says it, I believe it, that settles it." From my dad I heard, "The Church says so." To the frustration—and sometimes embarrassment—of both, my way seemed to be more about questioning than certainty. "Why?" was my never-ending refrain. I still recall my family trying to drag me away from an impromptu debate I was having with the monsignor immediately after Mass. It wasn't simply a matter of bucking authority; I genuinely wanted to dig deeper. It is no wonder that my favorite part of the Bible was the Psalter—the Book of Psalms—full of praises but also full of honest, heart-felt cries of anger and doubt.

Somewhere along the way, I left the church of my childhood, only to learn that I could not find an adequate substitute. Other places of worship, Christian or otherwise, had their own problems and limitations. As for people I knew who had left organized religion (a funny term) behind altogether, they often were as self-righteous and hypocritical as the religious folks they criticized! It was later, during a time of change in my life when any certainty I had was thrown out the window, that I first entered an Episcopal church and therein first opened The Book of Common Prayer.

I loved the service, and I appreciated the welcome from the people. I felt I had come home somehow. But it was the Prayer Book that really drew me in. Within a week, I asked if I could borrow a copy from the pews and take it home to read more carefully. In another week, I asked the priest where I could go to buy one for myself. In those earliest days, it was the earthiness of the Prayer Book that struck me the most. The words were beautiful and the religious themes clear, but throughout it all there was—there is—a sense that we encounter the Divine in the normal, ordinary things of life: water, bread, wine, ashes, oil, hands uplifted, hands laid on us, hands in blessing. The themes within speak not only of holiness but also of struggle, regret, and death—and hope. Others joke about the "pew aerobics" of standing, sitting, and kneeling throughout the services in the book, but I found the rhythms natural and appropriate.

It has been almost three decades since I first opened the pages of that special book, and I still find its words and rhythms so powerful, so absolutely necessary in my spiritual journey. I am a priest; more to the point, I am Canon to the Presiding Bishop of the Episcopal Church, which means I am something of an ambassador on the bishop's behalf both within and outside the church. Through it all, I find the Prayer Book to be my first and best tool, not to be used overtly by quoting its passages out of context like some dare to do with Holy Scripture. Rather, it serves as a source for my daily prayer and meditation, keeping me grounded so that I might be more fully prepared for whatever comes my way. And it offers spiritual gems that I can offer at special moments as needed.

So it is for many others, Anglican or otherwise, and so it has been for centuries now. This guide to the Prayer Book is intended to assist you—whether you are Anglican, a Christian from another tradition, or a fellow spiritual pilgrim wanting to explore this marvelous treasure chest. Before considering how to do that, however, it is helpful to engage in a little time travel. Let us look back through the centuries and explore the origins and the development of this book that continues to mean so much to so many.

The Heart of the New Church of England

The current American Book of Common Prayer was published in 1979, but its roots extend much further back to Tudor England, to the days of King Henry VIII. Though perhaps most famous for his ill-fated wives, Henry originally fancied himself something of a theologian. He is said, in fact, to have authored *In Defense of the Seven Sacraments*, a treatise attacking the Protestant reformer Martin Luther, for which the pope awarded the English monarch the title "Defender of the Faith" (a designation eventually bequeathed by Parliament to Henry's heirs). The king's break with Rome is at least ostensibly well known, though the situational complexities that led to the break—and the birth of the independent Church of England—are often ignored. It has been far easier for many to focus on Henry's anger against the pope for refusing the annulment he sought in order to pursue a second marriage.

There were other key factors that led to an independent Church of England, however, besides the king's need for an heir and his romance with Anne Boleyn. Increasing frustration had been developing for some time against perceived clerical abuses and financial corruption, including involuntary revenue assessments that put English money into Rome's coffers without consultation. This undisputed foreign authority was something that Henry would not abide.

In an amazingly short time, the king severed the ties that for centuries had bound his realm to the papacy and Roman Christianity. He closed down monasteries, allowed formerly celibate priests to get married and have children, and ordered all worship to be in English rather than Latin. No longer would his church be Roman Catholic.

Neither, however, would it be fully Protestant. The services were now in the language of the people, but they were still Catholic in form and feel. Monasteries were dissolved, but the monastic form of prayer left an indelible mark on what emerged. Henry bequeathed to his realm something familiar but new. The Church *in* England was evolving into the Church *of* England.

At the heart of this evolution was a work that would not be published until after Henry's death: The Book of Common Prayer. The original edition, published in 1549, was a remarkable work created for the most part by Thomas Cranmer, Henry's hand-selected Archbishop of Canterbury, the chief prelate in the English Church. It was Cranmer who, as a university scholar, first attracted Henry's attention when he offered a theological and political solution to the king's "privy matter," arguing that Henry did not need papal permission to divorce his first wife, Catherine of Aragon, and marry Anne Boleyn. What was needed, Cranmer asserted, was discussion with England's own theologians, who not only were learned but also sensitive to the needs of their own social and political milieu. Tradition was important, but so were local context and reason.

Thus, while others in continental Europe were making sweeping changes to Christian worship and organization, the reformation that spread across England's shores was more subtle ... but no less radical. The Prayer Book embodied these subtle yet radical changes. First and perhaps most importantly, it was written in English, not Latin. Worshippers and worship leaders alike used it; there was not a separate book for the clergy with their instructions on how to facilitate the liturgies. Those instructions, or rubrics, were in the one book shared by all. So although Cranmer retained bishops and priests, he bridged the gap between them and the laity by making sure that they all had access to the same resource and in a language that was "understood by the people." The BCP was therefore an empowering tool.

This BCP did not simply appear from thin air. It was, as its preface asserted, "grounded upon the holy scripture," and thanks to a thorough research of the works of the Apostolic Fathers, "agreeable to the order of the primitive Church." It incorporated Cranmer's own earlier writings, such as his Catechism and drafts for the Daily Office, as well as his Great Litany, produced during Henry's reign. It also was influenced by the many publications that had been promulgated in the years following Luther's break with Rome. German and Swiss orders, or forms for public services, had a noticeable impact on the English version of the Prayer Book, which was authorized for use by all the people of the realm through the Act of Conformity on the Feast of Pentecost, or Whitsunday, June 9, 1549.

Then—as now—there were people on either end of the theological and political spectrum who were not pleased with the book. It was too radical for those who sought to retain the old forms of worship, and too conservative for those who wanted bolder moves away from anything that appeared overly Catholic or "Romish." So it was soon thereafter that the first revision of the Prayer Book was published. The 1552 edition was more explicit in its rubrics, or explanatory instructions, and more in tune with some of the tenets of Calvinism, something that would have been unthinkable during Henry's reign, but which was encouraged by the Protestant advisors to Henry's sickly heir, Edward VI.

The new king's brief reign came to an end with the boy's death and his half-sister's rise to power. Interestingly, Henry had once sought permission from the pope to divorce Catherine of Aragon because the only surviving child she bore was female, and therefore by tradition unable to reign as Henry's heir. Yet now it was that same child, Mary, who took the throne and subsequently returned England to its Roman Catholic roots ... by force. Her nickname, Bloody Mary, was not bestowed on her by accident. Among those killed during her reign was Cranmer himself.

An unlikely martyr, the now-aged reformer actually recanted all his theological innovations after being imprisoned and tortured. He was no Martin Luther boldly declaring, "Here I stand, I can do no other!" No, Cranmer signed whatever they put before him, desperate to end the pain. It is, therefore, all the more incredible to witness the end of his story. When brought out before the crowds for his execution at the stake, Cranmer was invited to recant once more as an example to all the spectators. Instead, he shocked everyone (perhaps himself as well) by recanting his recantation! Cranmer's words have resounded through the years: "And forasmuch as my hand hath offended, writing contrary to my heart, my hand shall first be punished, for when I come to the fire, it shall be first burned." His courage at the end would be Cranmer's great legacy—that, of course, and the Prayer Book.

Features of Cranmer's Prayer Book

Three things are particularly noteworthy about Cranmer's Prayer Book. First, as briefly noted, it reveals his concern to wed reformed ideas to the basic structures of church worship. While there would be ongoing battles in the years ahead over specific issues like vestments or churchmanship, extremist departures from tradition at times found on the European continent were ameliorated by Cranmer's careful moderation. There would be criticism from the extreme ends of both sides about how far Cranmer had gone with the BCP, but the fact is that when one moves from the details to the big picture, the Prayer Book allowed England to retain its catholic, or universal, tradition of worship and sacraments while incorporating elements of the reformed faith that had become so important to him.

The second thing to note is how the Prayer Book encouraged a reforming movement that at its best would be marked more by common prayer than by common agreement. This seed would not fully blossom until the reign of Henry's daughter, Queen Elizabeth I, who famously remarked that she had no desire to "read into men's souls." How many sectarian movements then and now have demanded group-think, that all members sign on the dotted line? But the genius of the seed that Cranmer planted, and that came to full bloom under Elizabeth, is that communion and godly community need not be based on agreement on every theological point. Praying together was the key.

The third noteworthy thing about the Prayer Book is what it accomplished on the literary level. As mentioned already, it stands alongside the works of Shakespeare and the King James Bible in helping to reinvent and reinvigorate the English language, giving it both a breadth and a profound depth that had not previously been uncovered. It was not simply the vocabulary, but also the cadence and rhythm of the writing that made the BCP both exquisite and memorable.

Grounded in Holy Scripture, inheriting forms and structures from Roman and Lutheran liturgies, Cranmer went to a new level altogether in what he produced, opening with a preface that explains so clearly and yet so beautifully why such a work was needed and how its creation could be justified: "There was never any thing by the wit of man so well devised or so surely established, which (in continuance of time) hath not been corrupted."

It is quite possible to hear echoes of this acknowledgement of the need for change and ongoing development in the later provision for amendments in the Constitution of the United States. There was no question that rules were needed—the BCP was no libertarian document—but the rules that were set out were "few in number" and "plain and easy to understand." Thus did the same Prayer Book that developed from earlier sources become a catalyst for further development, so that "none other books [were needed] for their public service, but this book and the Bible."

Concerning the Prayer Book's approach to the scriptures, the 1549 book both reflected the Reformation's respect for the Bible and at the same time offered a more nuanced and contextual approach to scripture's complexities. It encouraged reading the entire Bible through the daily lectionary. One of the collects, or public prayers, in the 1549 book called on Christians to "read, mark, learn, and inwardly digest" the scriptures, not simply engage in subjective proof-texting. The BCP was therefore to be a book that theologically was grounded in scripture, that contained within itself large amounts of scripture, and that helped promote the reading of scripture in an orderly manner.

Order was a crucial matter for Elizabeth I when she succeeded her half-sister to the throne, having seen the dangers of excess and extremism during Mary's brief return of the nation to Roman Catholic ways. The new queen reintroduced the Prayer Book in a slightly revised form in 1559, and further small changes were made in 1637. Unfortunately, the order of the BCP and of the nation itself was soon torn asunder with the execution of King Charles I in 1649 and the beginning of Oliver Cromwell's rise to power. Only a century had passed since Cranmer's Prayer Book first arrived, and even less time since Elizabeth's golden age. Now, just as the monarchy was replaced with Cromwell's so-called Protectorate, so was the Prayer Book supplanted by his *Directory for Public Worship*.

The BCP's circuitous route took another turn with Cromwell's death and the end of his grand experiment. With the restoration of the monarchy in 1660 came the return of the Prayer Book, in the form of a new revision in 1662 that was closer to the original 1549 book. Though other revisions would later be proposed, the 1662 version has remained the official book for the Church of England to this day. In its preface, it affirmed once more the goal "to keep the mean between the two extremes," yet, ironically, over nine hundred clergy refused to accept it, giving birth to the so-called Nonconformist movement, a successor of sorts to the Puritans before.

It seems that the same Prayer Book that would give comfort, hope, and a sense of belonging to so many through the years would be too much for some and not enough for others.

A New Nation, a New Book

A little over another century passed before a new crisis—indeed, a revolution—resulted in a new Prayer Book for a new church in a new nation. "But when in the course of Divine Providence, these American States became independent with respect to civil government, their ecclesiastical independence was necessarily included." These words from the preface of the new American version of the BCP, ratified in Philadelphia in 1789, echoed the familiar words of the Declaration of Independence, penned in that same city in the summer of 1776. A mere thirteen years separated those two documents and yet, truly, the world had changed. The American Revolution changed it.

The beginnings of the American BCP are closely linked with the beginnings of the new nation. The Rev. Dr. William Smith of Maryland, who wrote the preface to that first American Prayer Book, was a friend and colleague of founding father Benjamin Franklin. The Rev. William White, who previously served as chaplain to the Continental Congress and later became the first presiding bishop of the Protestant Episcopal Church in the United States of America, focused his attention on creating a constitution for the newly independent body, arguing that it must "contain the constituent principles of the Church of England and yet be independent of foreign jurisdiction of influence."

Here again we see the emphasis on a middle way between breaking completely from the past and being bound by it. As stated in the 1783 document *Declaration of Certain Fundamental Rights and Liberties of the Protestant Episcopal Church of Maryland*, what was sought was only such revision as was needed to reflect "the change of our situation from a daughter to a sister Church." The desire was that, even as the church became independent, still there would be as much as possible a continuation of the doctrine, discipline, and worship of the Church of England, with any departures from that tradition being only what "local circumstances require."

Decision making in this new yet continuing church ultimately would rest not with a king or queen, or a parliament, or even an archbishop, but with the General Convention, the church's own legislative body composed of bishops, clergy, and, most remarkable, laypeople. In the years that followed, although it would never be the largest of the new country's Christian denominations, the church that both formed its Prayer Book and in turn was formed by it would become one of the most influential. In the early twentieth century Congress commissioned the construction of a national cathedral—and it was Episcopal. From George Washington to Franklin D. Roosevelt to George H. W. Bush, more than a quarter of all of our nation's chief executives have claimed the Episcopal Church as their own and worshipped using the Prayer Book.

That first American book, the 1789 BCP, included changes from earlier English versions, the most obvious ones concerning prayers for civil leaders, moving from "God save the King" to petitions for the president and members of Congress. The church's leadership in that early period also seized the opportunity to consider other alterations "uninfluenced and unrestrained by any worldly authority whatsoever." Other colonial churches would follow suit, as Prayer Book revision took place in Canada, Ireland, Scotland, and New Zealand, among other places.

The ongoing goal in Prayer Book revisions was, as nineteenth-century Episcopal priest William Reed Huntington described it, to provide "liturgical enrichment and increased flexibility of use." Enrichment and flexibility. Continuity and change. A century after the first American BCP came the 1892 version, then another revision in 1928. Innovations came in the decades following the First World War, as new discoveries of ancient scriptural and related texts resulted in a liturgical renaissance within various Christian traditions. The result for Episcopalians was the 1979 BCP. But the Episcopal Church is no longer simply American but multi-national and multi-ethnic. Spanish and French versions of the BCP have been introduced as well as various supplemental resources and hymnals, including *Enriching Our Worship*, *The Book of Occasional Services*, and *Holy Women, Holy Men*.

Many Nations, Many Books

The 1979 version of The Book of Common Prayer is only one of several different versions in the worldwide Anglican Communion, that global network of independent yet interdependent national or regionally based churches. The official Prayer Books in the Episcopal Church of Scotland, the Church of Ireland, the Anglican Church of Canada, and other places reflect the culture, the heritage, and the needs of those places.

Nowhere is this more evident than with the Prayer Book used in the Church of Aotearoa, New Zealand, and Polynesia, completed in 1989. There, the one church includes three distinct subgroups: the indigenous Māori people, the Pacific island peoples of Polynesia, and nonindigenous New Zealanders. Each subgroup has an archbishop, and the three take turns in representing the whole as primate of the entire church. Some speak of it as a mini-Anglican Communion, an intentionally creative way of honoring the different cultures and traditions of the various peoples therein.

That church's Prayer Book reflects this creative spirit in its multilingual and beautifully crafted language. As its own preface states, "It belongs to our environment and our people ... a gift from the Church to itself." This beautifully crafted Prayer Book is at times lyrical and uniquely memorable, a worthy successor to the Tudor-era Prayer Books.

Similarly, the Church of Ireland went through various revisions (in 1878 and 1926) before engaging in decades of research and reflection that resulted in the 2004 Irish Prayer Book. The goal, as stated in the book's preface, was nothing less than to "unify the worship of God's people, while allowing reasonable scope for diversity within the essential unity of the Church's prayer." As with other revisions throughout the world, those who worked on this sought to produce a book that would have "equal capacity to enrich private as well as corporate devotion."

The mother church of Anglicanism, the Church of England, took a different approach to all the new liturgical discoveries, retaining the 1662 BCP as the "permanently authorized" book for the church while adding a supplemental text in 2000 called *Common Worship: Services and Prayers for the Church of England*, a book that "reflects the multiplicity of contexts in which worship is offered today." It is an imaginative, wonderful tool for personal devotional use.

The Anglican Tradition Today

As we have seen, Cranmer's work centuries ago has taken root and blossomed in myriad ways. The Anglican tradition that has both given life to The Book of Common Prayer and been shaped by it remains a powerful outlet for the Christian gospel. While some traditions have opted to emphasize unanimity of thought, the Episcopal Church and other parts of the worldwide Anglican Communion have pointed to the importance of making room for disagreement. Where some Christian groups have offered easy answers, Episcopalians have affirmed the need to wrestle with the questions. It is not just the ultimate destination, but the spiritual journey itself that is to be honored and celebrated.

This is the keystone of the Episcopal Church, and of Anglicanism. We boldly affirm our place in the one, holy, catholic, and apostolic church, and we honor the traditions that we have inherited. Yet we have not been afraid to challenge those traditions when new understandings of God's reconciling work among us have become clear. In our worship, we look like Roman Catholics, and yet our priests and bishops can be married ... and many are women. On so many issues, we continue to find ourselves holding vastly different positions.

Yet at our best we dare to let go of our own infallibility of thought long enough to listen to the voice of one on the other side of the debate, and perhaps allow some room in our hearts to hear God in that opposing voice. As Desmond Tutu, Archbishop Emeritus of the Anglican Province of Southern Africa and Nobel Laureate, once described Anglicanism, it is "very messy, but also very loveable." Through it all, we pilgrims, so diverse in so many ways, continue to find our life together ... in common prayer.

A Key to the Treasure Chest

All this brings us to the important question of how to make use of The Book of Common Prayer. If you are an Episcopalian/Anglican, you may know well the section of the book devoted to the Holy Eucharist. Indeed, most Prayer Books in church pews have those pages weathered, while the rest of the book looks pristine, untouched. For you, this is a chance to explore those unexplored sections. If you know nothing more about the Episcopal Church or Anglicanism than what you have read here but want to go deeper in your devotional life, then this is a chance to draw on the riches therein and find nuggets of wisdom and holiness.

This guide serves as a key to unlock those treasures. As you turn the pages, the right side will have a passage taken directly from the Prayer Book, while the left side is devoted to annotations. Some of these notes are explanatory, clarifying the meaning of a particular term or the origin of an action or event listed. These notes are marked by a number, as with footnotes or endnotes in a document. The other notes are marked with a non-numerical symbol, as these are comments about the entire passage or personal reflections on that passage. My hope is that these two types of notes will aid you, whatever your tradition or interest, in accessing the wisdom of the BCP.

The chapters of this guide correspond with the ordering of the 1979 American Prayer Book, starting with "A Life of Prayer." This includes passages dealing with the rhythm of prayer throughout the year—the Church Calendar—and throughout the day—the Daily Office: Morning Prayer, Noon Prayer, Evening Prayer, and Compline (at the end of the night). It also includes selections from the Collects, or the prayers that collect the themes of each week in the Prayer Book cycle of scripture readings.

"Belonging and Building Relationships" addresses the key sacramental rites of Baptism and Eucharist—those parts of the BCP most familiar to Episcopalians/Anglicans—through which people can understand what it means to be children of God and members of God's family.

"Blessing in Times of Joy and Pain" focuses on the Pastoral Offices, that section of the Prayer Book that looks at rites of passage, repentance and reconciliation, marriage and children, sickness and death. How do we find the Divine Presence in such moments? Where is God when we laugh and when we weep?

"Called to Serve" includes passages from the Episcopal Services, those rites at which a bishop officiates, most notably the ordination of ministers and the consecration of sacred sites and objects. Here we consider our place in the larger whole, how we can make a difference in the world in which we live.

"Praise and Petition" includes selections from the Psalter, which is found in its entirety in the Prayer Book, as well as additional prayers and thanksgivings, some quite exquisite, yet often missed, since they are tucked away near the end of the BCP. This section also includes historical documents of the church and the Catechism, a Q&A model for approaching Anglican beliefs.

Finally, there is a brief concluding section I call "Using the Prayer Book as a Spiritual Tool."

Ultimately, it is my hope that by examining specific passages and exploring how it all fits together, you can indeed feel comfortable making The Book of Common Prayer a vital part of your spiritual journey.

As a final word: unless otherwise noted, passages covered in this guide are from the 1979 American version of The Book of Common Prayer (New York: Episcopal Church). When other versions of the BCP or supplemental texts are used, it will be noted. For Bible translations, unless otherwise noted, I have used the New Revised Standard Version (1989).

1 □ A Life of Prayer

The Prayer Book is steeped in a monastic heritage of daily prayer. Truly, if we go back much farther, we can say that the pattern of specific times of the day set for common prayer was born in ancient times, with prayers at the temple in Jerusalem in the morning, afternoon, and evening, and the early Christians beginning and ending each day with corporate prayer.

By the late Middle Ages, monks had developed an elaborate system that included prayers at midnight or cockcrow (Matins), early morning (Lauds), the first hour (Prime), the third hour or 9 a.m. (Terce), the sixth hour or noon (Sext), the ninth hour or 3 p.m. (None), dusk (Vespers), and bedtime (Compline). Ordinary Christians were separate from all of this, as it was seen as the work of the monks.

Thomas Cranmer, in his 1549 Book of Common Prayer, simplified the system into Matins (eventually just called Morning Prayer) and Evensong. In the Episcopal Church, Morning Prayer was the principal Sunday service in most congregations, with Eucharist held only every other week or even just once a month. Lay leaders could officiate at Morning Prayer as easily as clergy. With the arrival of the 1979 Book of Common Prayer, the Eucharist became the primary Sunday service, and Morning Prayer is now only rarely used in congregations.

However, along with Noon Prayer, Evening Prayer, and Compline, the Prayer Book has become a widely used tool for individuals in their own devotional life. Using one or more of these services along with the Daily Office Lectionary at the back of the Prayer Book, you can read through the Bible systematically in the context of personal prayer and reflection. There is Rite I with traditional language and Rite II with contemporary wording. The Daily Office is a daily discipline, indeed a spiritual gift, cherished by many.

❖ Ours is a 24/7 culture. We buy, eat, and travel around the clock. As a greater number of people work two or more jobs to make ends meet, days begin to meld together, so that one day feels like any other.

The Prayer Book offers a different way of understanding time and our place in it. Placed at the very start of the book, the Church Calendar reminds us of the importance of cycles and seasons, times of celebration and times of penitence.

Time matters because we matter. Ours is not some arbitrary existence. We are beloved of God, and the days and seasons of our lives are all part of the divine design.

1 The change of the principal day of common worship from Saturday, the Sabbath, to the first day of the week in commemoration of Christ's resurrection is one of the most radical changes made by the early Christians. Sundays, also referred to as the Lord's Day, are considered "mini-Easters."

2 The 1979 Prayer Book introduced special liturgies for Ash Wednesday and Good Friday, and although not as widely observed as in previous eras, many people still fast on these days. Likewise, some still abstain from eating meat on Fridays, especially during Lent. While the practice may seem quaint to some, it is a form of spiritual self-discipline that adherents say brings great benefits.

The Church Year consists of two cycles of feasts and holy days: one is dependent upon the moveable date of the Sunday of the Resurrection or Easter Day; the other, upon the fixed date December 25, the Feast of our Lord's Nativity or Christmas Day.

All Sundays of the year are feasts of our Lord Jesus Christ.[1]

The following days are observed by special acts of discipline and self-denial: Ash Wednesday and the other weekdays of Lent and of Holy Week, except the feast of Annunciation, and Good Friday and all other Fridays of the year, in commemoration of the Lord's crucifixion.[2]

FROM THE CALENDAR OF THE CHURCH YEAR

❖ Every person is special and has the potential to make a difference in the world, in small ways or great. The persons listed in the Church Calendar are simply models for us all, taken from various times and places, all witnesses of the love of God. The recent supplemental text *Holy Women, Holy Men* expands the list and offers short biographies along with scripture readings and a prayer.

If ever we feel disconnected from these heroes of the faith, we might well remember these words from the hymn "I Sing a Song of the Saints of God": "They lived not only in ages past, there are hundreds of thousands still ... for the saints of God are just folk like me, and I mean to be one too."

3 The date assigned to each person included in the Church Calendar is the date of that person's death, or rather, the date of that person's new birth into eternity, the larger life.

4 Those listings that are in bold mark Major Feasts associated with our Lord or with Mary, the apostles, the writers of the Gospels, and other key figures, as well as national days such as Independence Day and Thanksgiving. In earlier Prayers Books, these were differentiated from the so-called Lesser Feasts, the commemorations of various holy women and men throughout the centuries, by being colored in red. From this eventually came a popular tradition of referring to special days in one's life as "red-letter days."

August

10 Laurence, Deacon, and Martyr at Rome, 258[3]

11 Clare, Abbess at Assisi, 1253

12 Florence Nightengale, Nurse, Social Reformer, 1910

13 Jeremy Taylor, Bishop of Down, Connor, and Dromore, 1667

14 Jonathan Myrick Daniels, Seminarian and Witness for Civil Rights, 1965

15 **Saint Mary the Virgin, Mother of Our Lord Jesus Christ[4]**

FROM THE CALENDAR OF THE CHURCH YEAR

❖ From Cranmer on, it has been important to have confession be done in the context of knowing that God abounds in mercy. In this way, confession is not pleading with an unforgiving deity, but rather owning up to the reality about ourselves, that we have indeed sinned.

Together with the absolution that follows, this is a perfect way to begin and end a day. It is no accident that this confession, or a shortened form of it, is found not only in Morning Prayer, but in Noon Prayer, Evening Prayer, and Compline as well. It is a healthy thing to stop and take stock of ourselves, and a wonderful thing to be reminded that we are absolved, forgiven, free to start anew as many times as is needed.

5 Because the confession, like other prayers in the Prayer Book, is intended primarily for public or "common" prayer, the plural pronoun is used. But this prayer, like others that follow throughout the book, is easily adapted for personal use, as in, "I have not loved you with my whole heart; I have not loved my neighbors as myself. I am truly sorry and I humbly repent."

6 The BCP is clear that we need to repent not only of things that we have done, but also of things that we have failed to do, whether for lack of courage or lack of concern. There is an echo here of the familiar proverb that evil can succeed only when good people do nothing.

7 The absolution of sins is a powerful spiritual concept that in Western culture dates back to the early days of Judaism. An animal—a scapegoat—was sacrificed on behalf of the people, their sins having been symbolically transferred to that animal. For Christians, Jesus, the Son of God, willingly became the Lamb of God, whose sacrifice on the cross made possible the forgiveness of sins.

Most merciful God,
We[5] confess that we have sinned against you
in thought, word, and deed,
by what we have done,
and by what we have left undone.[6]
We have not loved you with our whole heart;
we have not loved our neighbors as ourselves.
We are truly sorry and we humbly repent.
For the sake of your Son Jesus Christ,
have mercy on us and forgive us;
that we may delight in your will,
and walk in your ways,
to the glory of your Name. Amen.

Almighty God have mercy on you, forgive you all your sins
through our Lord Jesus Christ, strengthen you in all goodness, and by the power of the Holy Spirit keep you in eternal life. Amen.[7]

THE CONFESSION AND ABSOLUTION, FROM DAILY MORNING PRAYER II

❖ The Invitatory and Psalter follows the confession and precedes our reading of the scripture lessons for the day. It is, as the name suggests, an invitation to praise God.

How important it is to take a moment in our busy lives—amidst our planning and working and fretting and fearing—and acknowledge that God is still God, so we don't have to try to be.

8 The Gloria Patri—literally, Glory to the Father—dates back in an earlier form to the fourth century and is used here as a distinctly trinitarian bookend before and after the appointed psalms, many of which were written a thousand years before the coming of Christ.

9 This is the first of many reminders in the Prayer Book that we refrain from saying "Alleluia" in the season of Lent, as a reminder of the realities of our own sin and need for repentance. But for the rest of the year we are bold to say, "Alleluia," even as Cranmer's 1549 book said, "Praise ye the Lord!"

10 The first half of the antiphons—brief scriptural verses that precede the psalms for the day—change, reflecting the themes of the church's seasons, but all call on us to come and adore our Creator and Redeemer.

11 The psalms are assigned in such a way that you read through the entire Psalter every seven weeks. They are preceded by either the Venite, listed here, or the Jubilate, two particular psalms of praise.

Lord, open our lips.
And our mouth shall proclaim your praise.

Glory to the Father, and to the Son, and to the Holy Spirit;
as it was in the beginning, is now, and will be for ever.
Amen.[8]

[*Except in Lent, add*] Alleluia.[9]

Worship the Lord in the beauty of holiness: Come let us
adore him.[10]

Come, let us sing to the Lord;
    let us shout for joy to the Rock of our salvation.
Let us come before his presence with thanksgiving
    and raise a loud shout to him with psalms.[11]

THE INVITATORY AND PSALTER, FROM DAILY MORNING PRAYER II

❖ Canticles are songs of praise that follow the Christian scripture readings during Morning or Evening Prayer, just as the Psalms follow the Hebrew scripture readings.

The First Song of Isaiah is well over two thousand years old, yet still its words give hope, strength, and comfort for anyone who needs help, who is willing to trust God and not give in to fear. The "I/my" pronouns soon turn to "you/your" as if this is a conversation between God and me. As I dare to proclaim my trust, dare to acknowledge that the Lord is my sure defense, then God responds and assures me that I will one day give thanks, and not only I, but all the faithful people of God, all who are, as it were, spiritual inhabitants of Zion.

Yes, the going is tough sometimes, but God is right there with me, right there with you, and so I can indeed choose to trust, to not fear, to give thanks.

12 As with the psalms, canticles used in worship conclude with the Gloria Patri, a reminder that all our prayers and praises are grounded in our relationship with the Divine One, who is relational to the very core.

Surely, it is God who saves me;
  I will trust in him and not be afraid.
For the Lord is my stronghold and my sure defense,
  and he will be my Savior.
Therefore you shall draw water with rejoicing
  from the springs of salvation.
And on that day you shall say,
  Give thanks to the Lord and call upon his Name;
Make his deeds known among the peoples;
  see that they remember that his Name is exalted.
Sing the praises of the Lord, for he has done great things,
  and this is known in all the world.
Cry aloud, inhabitants of Zion, ring out your joy,
  for the great one in the midst of you is the Holy One of
  Israel.

Glory to the Father, and to the Son, and to the Holy Spirit:
as it was in the beginning, is now, and will be for ever.
Amen.[12]

CANTICLE 9, FIRST SONG OF ISAIAH, FROM DAILY MORNING PRAYER II

❖ The Apostles' Creed is an ancient profession predating the familiar Nicene Creed that is used weekly in the Eucharist. The 1549 Prayer Book instructed that the minister was to "say the Creed and the Lord's Prayer in English, with a loud voice," as contrasted with the silent recitations in medieval services. With the 1552 revision of the BCP, the people joined in reciting the creed.

The creed is our personal profession of faith—"I believe"—and the Lord's Prayer our ensuing request for forgiveness and "daily bread" from the God in whom we put our faith and trust.

Because I believe, I dare to ask God for help. Because I believe, I dare to forgive and be forgiven. Because I believe, I dare to call myself a child of God, who is my Father, my Mother, my Creator, and my Redeemer.

13 This mention of Pontius Pilate, a first-century Roman overseer of the Palestine region, sets the creed in the world of history. The story of Jesus is not simply some timeless myth; it is about someone who lived and died, and who Christians proclaim was resurrected, in real time, "under Pontius Pilate."

14 The original version of the creed said, "He descended to hell," a reference to the story that before Christ arose on Easter morning, he fought to free the souls of those faithful people who had been in Hades, the underworld, awaiting his coming.

15 The un-capitalized word "catholic" means universal, not Roman Catholic.

16 All four Gospel writers as well as Saint Paul proclaim not just a spiritual but a bodily resurrection for Christ. Because Jesus was raised and given a new body, Paul said in 1 Corinthians 15, we can trust that we too will one day receive a new, risen body.

I believe in God, the Father almighty,
   creator of heaven and earth.
I believe in Jesus Christ, his only Son, our Lord.
   He was conceived by the power of the Holy Spirit
   and born of the Virgin Mary,
   He suffered under Pontius Pilate,[13]
   was crucified, died, and was buried.
   He descended to the dead.[14]
   On the third day he rose again.
   He ascended into heaven,
   and is seated
   at the right hand of the Father.
   He will come again to judge the living and the dead.
I believe in the Holy Spirit,
   the holy catholic Church,[15]
   the communion of saints,
   the forgiveness of sins,
   the resurrection of the body,[16]
   and the life everlasting. Amen.

THE APOSTLES' CREED, FROM DAILY MORNING PRAYER II

❖ Prayer is not about rubbing a lamp so that a genie can pop out and grant three wishes. It is about viewing the needs of the world through the lens of God's love and thereby becoming a prayerful people.

Every morning, whether on our own or with others, we can offer our prayers to the God who is bigger than we. In doing so, we allow the prayer to touch and transform us. For even as we pray that the needy will not be forgotten, we are in a real sense allowing the Spirit of God to soften our own hearts, that we might not forget the needy whom we encounter. Even as we pray that God's way may be known upon the earth, we are the instruments by which that way may be made known.

17 Suffrages are intercessory petitions and originally in the Middle Ages referred to intercessions on behalf of the dead. The word comes from the Latin *suffragium,* meaning aid or assistance.

18 Earlier suffrages, as well as collects, from the Church of England acknowledged the monarch and the royal family. Of course, following the American Revolution, this was something the newly independent States no longer did. It was precisely passages like this that led to the creation of the 1789 American book.

V. Show us your mercy, O Lord;
R. And grant us your salvation.
V. Clothe your ministers with righteousness;
R. Let your people sing with joy.
V. Give peace, O Lord, in all the world;
R. For only in you can we live in safety.
V. Lord, keep this nation under your care;
R. And guide us in the way of justice and truth.
V. Let your way be known upon earth;
R. Your saving health among all nations.
V. Let not the needy, O Lord, be forgotten;
R. Nor the hope of the poor be taken away.
V. Create in us clean hearts, O God;
R. And sustain us with your Holy Spirit.

SUFFRAGES A,[17] FROM DAILY MORNING PRAYER II

V. O Lord, shew thy mercy upon us.
R. And grant us thy salvation.
V. O Lord, save the Queen.[18]
R. And mercifully hear us when we call upon thee.

FROM THE BOOK OF COMMON PRAYER, 1662

❖ A new day means a new start, new possibilities, new hope. Whatever happened yesterday or last week or last year is past. Each new
sunrise is a divine gift, a chance to start anew, to continue the good
things already in progress, to be rid of the things that get in the way of
our becoming all that we can truly be as God's beloved.

None of this happens by sheer will. We need not face "all the cares
and occupations of our life" on our own. The Almighty One, the one in
whom "we live and move and have our being," is with us to preserve
us, to protect us, to strengthen us. We have only to seek, and we will
find that companion, right there with us, each day, every day.

19 A collect is a focused prayer that collects our thoughts and intentions
toward a particular theme. Each Sunday's collect, for example, ties in
to the scripture readings assigned to that day, so that there is continuity in what we read and pray.

20 This prayer comes from the Canadian Prayer Book of 1922, where it
was entitled "For Remembrance of God's Presence." Its origins before
that are lost in the centuries.

Lord God, almighty and everlasting Father, you have brought us in safety to this new day: Preserve us with your mighty power, that we may not fall into sin, nor be overcome by adversity; and in all we do, direct us to the fulfilling of your purpose; through Jesus Christ our Lord. Amen.[19]

COLLECT FOR GRACE, FROM DAILY MORNING PRAYER II

Heavenly Father, in you we live and move and have our being: We humbly pray you so to guide and govern us by your Holy Spirit, that in all the cares and occupations of our life we may not forget you, but may remember that we are ever walking in your sight; through Jesus Christ our Lord. Amen.[20]

COLLECT FOR GUIDANCE, FROM DAILY MORNING PRAYER II

❖ The English writer G. K. Chesterton once said, "When it comes to life the critical thing is whether you take things for granted or take them with gratitude." How easy it is to take things for granted and to pray to God only when we need something or are frustrated with the way things are.

This is why the prayer known as the General Thanksgiving is so important. Coming at the end of our prayers and petitions, it is a way of admitting how much we have for which to be grateful.

We can choose to be miserable, as some indeed do, complaining about all that they don't have in life. Or we can choose to give thanks to God for the gifts we do have, "our creation, preservation, and all the blessings of this life," including, of course, our redemption in Christ.

For this reason, the General Thanksgiving was added to the Prayer Book in 1662, and remains in the 1979 BCP.

21 It has been suggested that this first part of the prayer was adapted from a private prayer of Queen Elizabeth I at the end of the 1500s.

22 Our thankfulness shows itself chiefly not in what we say with our lips, but in how we live. Faithful lives are our best expression of gratefulness.

Almighty God, Father of all mercies,
we your unworthy servants give you humble thanks
for all your goodness and loving-kindness
to us and to all whom you have made.
We bless you for our creation, preservation,
and all the blessings of this life;[21]
but above all for your immeasurable love
in the redemption of the world by our Lord Jesus Christ;
for the means of grace, and for the hope of glory.
And, we pray, give us such an awareness of your mercies,
that with truly thankful hearts we may show forth your praise,
not only with our lips, but in our lives,
by giving up our selves to your service,[22]
and by walking before you
in holiness and righteousness all our days;
through Jesus Christ our Lord,
to whom, with you and the Holy Spirit,
be honor and glory throughout all ages. Amen.

THE GENERAL THANKSGIVING FROM DAILY MORNING PRAYER II

❖ The suggested lessons for Noonday are short by intention, fitting into a busy day while giving us a moment to breathe, a moment to reflect on things heavenly in the midst of our daily bombardment by things earthly.

23 This first verse draws from Romans 5:5, part of a passage dealing with justification by faith and the hope of glory. This hope, as the verse immediately preceding it makes clear, ultimately comes out of the ongoing suffering that we endure. Endurance produces character, Paul says, which in turn results in hope ... hope that does not disappoint. And why not? Because, Paul says, that hope, like the faith with which it is linked, is forever grounded in that love that "has been poured into our hearts," that "Love divine," as Charles Wesley's familiar hymn describes it, "all loves excelling."

24 These well-known verses from 2 Corinthians 5:17–18 are part of a larger passage that opens with Paul claiming to "walk by faith, not by sight" (5:7). How we get through our daily life, how we view every-thing and everyone around us, makes all the difference in the world. John Wesley once challenged his listeners to ask themselves, "What am I seeking day by day ... the things that are seen, or the things that are not seen?" If only we will open our eyes, we will see God's new creation.

25 The third reading, from Malachi 1:11, reflects the idea that prayer and praises are to be offered throughout the day, from sunrise to sun-down, and specifically points to the importance of the Name of God being lifted up. "Lord of Hosts" was a descriptor that denoted God's authority over angelic or heavenly hosts.

The love of God has been poured into our hearts through the Holy Spirit that has been given to us.[23]
Thanks be to God.

If anyone is in Christ he is a new creation; the old has passed away, behold the new has come. All this is from God, who through Christ reconciled us to himself and gave us the ministry of reconciliation.[24]
Thanks be to God.

From the rising of the sun to its setting my Name shall be great among the nations, and in every place incense shall be offered to my Name, and a pure offering; for my Name shall be great among the nations, says the Lord of Hosts.[25]
Thanks be to God.

SCRIPTURE READINGS, FROM AN ORDER OF SERVICE FOR NOONDAY

❖ These prayers from the Noonday Service reflect an ancient tradition dating back to the second century that encouraged brief, more private prayer services during the day between the familiar Matins (Morning Prayer) and Vespers (Evening Prayer). These other "little offices," at 9 a.m., noon, 3 p.m. (Terce, Sext, None), were meant to draw prayerful attention to mission through the lens of Christ's Passion or Saint Paul's conversion.

26 This prayer calls to mind the words of Jesus in John 12:32, "I, when I am lifted up from the earth, will draw all people to myself." Through the Passion of Christ, all people can find their redemption. Composed in the nineteenth century, the prayer speaks poignantly and beautifully of the Savior's "loving arms" and "tender mercies." What an image of divine love: stretching, reaching, holding us close to the very heart of God.

27 In the Acts of the Apostles, chapter 9, we read the story of Paul, a persecutor of early Christians who saw their savior as a threat to the carefully constructed religious boundaries that separated faithful Jews from pagan Gentiles. How ironic then that God would call Paul to be the chief witness to those same Gentiles whom he previously had avoided at all costs. The mention of illumining the world may tie in with Isaiah 9, which speaks of the people who lived in darkness suddenly seeing a great light.

28 This prayer, also found in the Roman Catholic Mass following the Lord's Prayer, speaks of the peace that Christ has offered to us and that we in turn are called to share with one another and with all those we encounter. The words of Jesus come from John 14:27.

Blessed Savior, at this hour you hung upon the cross, stretching out your loving arms: Grant that all the peoples of the earth may look to you and be saved; for your tender mercies' sake. Amen.[26]

Almighty Savior, who at noonday called your servant Saint Paul to be an apostle to the Gentiles: We pray you to illumine the world with the radiance of your glory, that all nations may come and worship you; for you live and reign for ever and ever. Amen.[27]

Lord Jesus Christ, you said to your apostles, "Peace I give to you; my own peace I leave with you:" Regard not our sins, but the faith of your Church, and give to us the peace and unity of that heavenly City, where with the Father and the Holy Spirit you live and reign, now and for ever. Amen.[28]

THE COLLECTS, FROM AN ORDER OF SERVICE FOR NOONDAY

29 The *Phos Hilaron* is an ancient prayer of light, the earliest known Christian hymn recorded outside the Bible. Already considered an old and cherished hymn by the time of Saint Basil the Great, who in the mid-300s mentions its use, it was first translated into English in 1834 by John Keble with the opening line "Hail, gladdening Light, of his pure glory poured." Subsequent translations included one by poet Henry Wadsworth Longfellow.

Said or sung at the time of Vespers, or evening prayers, it is a bright and hopeful prayer, looking to the Light of Christ even as the natural lights of the day are beginning to ebb.

30 The *Magnificat* is Mary's lyrical response in the Gospel of Luke when her cousin Elizabeth commends her for her willingness to give birth to the Messiah. Luke includes three other hymns of praise in the early chapters of his Gospel: Zechariah's *Benedictus*, the angels' *Gloria in Excelsis*, and Simeon's *Nunc Dimitis*. All may be found in the 1979 BCP.

Mary's hymn resembles the prayer of Hannah, the mother of Samuel in 1 Samuel 2:1–10. Like that earlier song of praise, Mary's canticle is at once joy-filled and humble. It is "the greatness of the Lord," not Mary's own worthiness, that is at the heart of this canticle, and because of that, it is the song of anyone who has reason to offer thanks to God for grace in their life.

Cranmer's 1549 Prayer Book had this as the only canticle used after the first lesson was read during Evensong. The contemporary translation, like many other texts in the 1979 BCP, comes from the International Consultation on English Texts (ICET).

O gracious Light,
pure brightness of the everliving Father in heaven,
O Jesus Christ, holy and blessed!

Now as we come to the setting of the sun,
and our eyes behold the vesper light,
we sing your praises, O God: Father, Son, and Holy Spirit.

You are worthy at all times to be praised by happy voices,
O Son of God, O Giver of life,
and to be glorified through all the worlds.[29]

PHOS HILARON, FROM DAILY EVENING PRAYER II

My soul proclaims the greatness of the Lord,
my spirit rejoices in God my Savior;
    for he has looked with favor on his lowly servant.
From this day all generations will call me blessed:
    the Almighty has done great things for me,
    and holy is his Name.[30]

THE MAGNIFICAT, FROM DAILY EVENING PRAYER II

❖ This series of short petitions leads us from the busyness of the day into an evening that we pray will be "holy, good, and peaceful." As part of the larger Evening Prayer service, these suffrages speak of the need for peace in many ways and on many levels: a peaceful night, paths of peace, the peace that comes from forgiveness, peace for the church, peace for the world, peace of mind as we face our own mortality.

In the Gospels, the Risen Christ assured his followers of the gift of a peace that is more than the world can give. "Peace I leave with you" (John 14:27). Peace is so much more than the cessation of conflict or the absence of problems. The peace that we find in the divine embrace is, as Saint Paul once described it, a peace that "surpasses all understanding" (Philippians 4:7).

That is the kind of peace to which these evening petitions point. It is not about everything being well right now; things may be anything but well right now. But, like the fourteenth-century English mystic Julian of Norwich once said, in praying, in coming to God with our needs and the needs of the world around us, we can begin to know deep in our hearts that in God's time and in God's love "all shall be well, and all shall be well, and all manner of things shall be well."

So, we can dare to close our evening with these simple, yet profound petitions. Let there be peace. We entreat you, O Lord.

31 These suffrages, first included in the 1979 BCP, are based on the concluding litany used in Eastern Orthodox evening services.

That this evening may be holy, good, and peaceful,
We entreat you, O Lord.

That your holy angels may lead us in paths of peace and
goodwill,
We entreat you, O Lord.

That we may be pardoned and forgiven for our sins and
offenses,
We entreat you, O Lord.

That there may be peace to your Church and to the whole
world,
We entreat you, O Lord.

That we may depart this life in your faith and fear, and not
be condemned before the great judgment seat of Christ,
We entreat you, O Lord.

That we may be bound together by your Holy Spirit in the
communion of all your saints, entrusting one another and
all our life to Christ,
We entreat you, O Lord.[31]

SUFFRAGES B, FROM EVENING PRAYER II

[32] This prayer was first included in the 1928 BCP and is something of a hodgepodge of different pieces meshed into one collect. The preamble is a series of descriptors for God, showing how we encounter the Divine One in different ways, depending on where we are in our journey: light and life, strength and repose, but always the same God. With its final request about bringing us in safety to the morning hours, this prayer stands as a nice bookend to the Collect for Grace in Morning Prayer, with its opening, "You have brought us in safety to this new day."

[33] In Luke 24:13–35, we read of two disciples who, following Jesus's crucifixion, find themselves distraught and dejected as they journey on the road to Emmaus. Along the way, they encounter a stranger, who asks about their sorrow and proceeds to lift their spirits. Coming to the end of the day, they invite the stranger to join them in a nearby inn to share a meal with them, and as he breaks the bread and shares it with him, they recognize the Risen Christ. As dusk signals the end of a long day of toil, and perhaps an even longer night of regret and worry, we, like those two disciples, may find ourselves in need of a companion, someone to give hope where there is none, someone to light a fire in us.

[34] This collect from the New Zealand BCP also speaks of God's presence with us: "Be with us still." This petition comes in the context of a life of gratitude. As evening comes, we look back over all that God has done for us that day, and we give thanks. As we give thanks, we also commend ourselves once more, and not only ourselves but also those we love, to the same gracious God who has done so much for us already.

O God, the life of all who live, the light of the faithful, the strength of those who labor, and the repose of the dead: We thank you for the blessings of the day that is past, and humbly ask you for your protection through the coming night. Bring us in safety to the morning hours; through him who died and rose again for us, your Son our Savior Jesus Christ. Amen.[32]

COLLECT FOR PROTECTION, FROM DAILY EVENING PRAYER II

Lord Jesus, stay with us, for evening is at hand and the day is past; be our companion in the way, kindle our hearts, and awaken hope, that we may know you as you are revealed in Scripture and the breaking of bread. Grant this for the sake of your love. Amen.[33]

COLLECT FOR THE PRESENCE OF CHRIST, FROM DAILY EVENING PRAYER II

Gracious God, you have given us much today; grant us also a thankful spirit. Into your hands we commend ourselves and those we love. Be with us still, and when we take our rest renew us for the service of your Son Jesus Christ. Amen.[34]

COLLECT FOR THE EVENING,
FROM THE 1989 NEW ZEALAND PRAYER BOOK

❖ We are all interconnected. We need each other. Yet how easy it is to forget all the ways in which our lives are enhanced by one another and how we encounter the grace of God through one another. With these prayers from two church Fathers, we are reminded that we can never be content to focus only on ourselves, but must allow God's own ever-expanding love to fill us and overflow through us.

35 This collect comes from Saint Augustine of Hippo, the famed theologian, bishop, and Doctor of the Church who lived and wrote in the early part of the fifth century. The prayer is both beautiful and beloved by many, displaying God's gentle love, ever ready to meet people in all their various situations and needs. The line "shield the joyous" is one that is particularly poignant and has many scriptural precedents, including Psalm 3:3, "But you, O Lord, are a shield around me, my glory, and the one who lifts up my head."

36 With its mention of the promise from Matthew's Gospel, we see here that the Divine Presence can be found whenever two or more are gathered together in the name of Christ. It also reminds us to be confident that God is ever ready to respond to our desires and petitions, but only "as may be best for us."

37 This prayer was included by Cranmer in his English Litany in 1544, a first step toward his 1549 Prayer Book, and was recognized as being attributed to early church father John Chrysostom, whose name literally means "golden-tongued" or "golden-mouthed." Its title was given in the 1662 English BCP, still the official version of the Prayer Book in the Church of England. It was the prayer that closed both Morning and Evening Prayer.

Keep watch, dear Lord, with those who work, or watch, or weep this night, and give your angels charge over those who sleep. Tend the sick, Lord Christ; give rest to the weary, bless the dying, soothe the suffering, pity the afflicted, shield the joyous; and all for your love's sake. Amen.[35]

COLLECT FOR MISSION, FROM DAILY EVENING PRAYER II

Almighty God, you have given us grace at this time with one accord to make our common supplication to you; and you have promised through your well-beloved Son that when two or three are gathered together in his Name you will be in the midst of them: Fulfill now, O Lord, our desires and petitions as may be best for us; granting us in this world knowledge of your truth, and in the age to come life everlasting. Amen.[36]

PRAYER OF ST. CHRYSOSTOM,[37] FROM DAILY EVENING PRAYER RITE II

❖ The service of Compline dates back to the fourth century, as a time of prayer for the monks in their dormitories before going to sleep. Saint Benedict of Nursia mentioned Compline in his famed Rule, and while Thomas Cranmer did not include it as a separate service in the 1549 BCP, he did incorporate several of its parts into his service for Evensong. It has become a much beloved service for groups on retreats as well as for individuals.

38 The first versicle and response come originally from Psalm 31:5. Jesus quoted the first part while on the cross in Luke 23:46, and Stephen, the first Christian martyr, paraphrases it in Acts 7:59–60 when he calls on Jesus to receive his spirit. The prayer bespeaks an intimacy and trust that is particularly appropriate as we prepare for the night's sleep. The second versicle and response, from Psalm 17:8, is all about the protection and support we find in God in the face of all manner of assaults and incriminations. Alone at night, we look to the One who truly stands with us.

39 This very poignant collect dates back to medieval liturgies and prior to the 1979 BCP was included in the English, Scottish, and Canadian Compline services. It is hard not to let out a sigh as you speak of being "wearied by the changes and chances of this life."

40 Originally found in the Roman Catholic breviary (literally, a little or concise book which clergy used for their daily prayers), this is a petition for protection in the place of our rest. Wherever we are going to lay our heads, let that place be a place of peace.

41 This antiphon both precedes and follows the reading of the *Nunc Dimittis*, the Song of Simeon, which speaks of letting go. We are able to rest in peace because God is guiding and guarding us.

The Lord Almighty grant us a peaceful night and a perfect end. Amen.

V. Into your hands, O Lord, I commend my spirit;
R. For you have redeemed me, O Lord, O God of truth.
V. Keep us, O Lord, as the apple of your eye;
R. Hide us under the shadow of your wings.[38]

Be present, O merciful God, and protect us through the hours of this night, so that we who are wearied by the changes and chances of this life may rest in your eternal changelessness; through Jesus Christ our Lord. Amen.[39]

Visit this place, O Lord, and drive far from it all snares of the enemy; let your holy angels dwell with us to preserve us in peace; and let your blessing be upon us always; through Jesus Christ our Lord. Amen.[40]

Guide us waking, O Lord, and guard us sleeping; that awake we may watch with Christ, and asleep we may rest in peace.[41]

FROM AN ORDER FOR COMPLINE

❖ A litany is a series of short petitions followed by responses. The Great Litany, so named because there are other litanies in the BCP, was first produced by Thomas Cranmer in 1544 and included prayers taken from various medieval sources as well as some new material. After an initial invocation of the Blessed Trinity—Father, Son, and Holy Spirit—the service is divided into three main sections: the first being the deprecations, petitions for deliverance from sin and suffering of all types; the second being the intercessions for the church, the world, and all those in need; and the third being the Lord's Prayer and concluding collect.

In many ways, this litany served as a first step toward the creation just five years later of Cranmer's 1549 Prayer Book. The back and forth rhythmic quality of the litany is possible to feel even when read alone.

42 Cranmer based this lengthy invocation on Joel 2:17 and Tobit 3:3 (from the writings known as the Apocrypha, included in Anglican as well as Roman Catholic Bibles). It is a call for the Lord to spare us from our just deserts.

43 To many people today, these words may seem outdated or even offensive, as we do not speak much about sin and judgment, and fire-and-brimstone sermons are for the most part rare and unwelcome. Yet when the door is locked and we are completely alone, we may find ourselves still wrestling with a sense of guilt and terrible responsibility for our personal failings. In such moments, these words can actually feel somewhat liberating, admitting the worst while affirming that God loves us.

44 If there is one thing that we all share, it is our mortality. We will all die one day, though for most of us, we hope that "one day" will be far off in the future. This petition, which in its original form read, "from sudden death," now underscores the need for us never to find ourselves unprepared for death whenever it comes.

O holy, blessed, and glorious Trinity, one God,
Have mercy upon us.

Remember not, Lord Christ, our offenses, nor the offenses
of our forefathers; neither reward us according to our sins.
Spare us, good Lord, spare thy people, whom thou hast
redeemed with thy most precious blood, and may thy
mercy preserve us for ever.[42]
Spare us, good Lord.

From all evil and wickedness; from sin; from the crafts and
assaults of the devil; and from everlasting damnation,[43]
Good Lord, deliver us.

From all oppression, conspiracy, and rebellion; from vio-
lence, battle, and murder; and from dying suddenly and
unprepared,[44]
Good Lord, deliver us.

That it may please thee to support, help, and comfort all
who are in danger, necessity, and tribulation,
We beseech thee to hear us, good Lord.

Son of God, we beseech thee to hear us.
Son of God, we beseech thee to hear us.

FROM THE GREAT LITANY

❖ The Collects for the Church Year are selected in conjunction with the scripture readings for each particular Sunday or Feast Day, so that there is a theme that carries through each service. The three collects here are taken from three different liturgical seasons: Advent, Epiphany, and Easter.

45 This prayer was first found in the 1549 BCP, based on Romans 13:11–14, which is read on the first Sunday of Advent in the church calendar. Beginning with the 1662 Prayer Book, it was to be used not just on the first day of Advent, but every day throughout the season.

It speaks of us living in this in-between time, "now," with Christ's first advent or coming behind us and his second coming still to come. In this time we are called, with divine grace empowering us, to "cast away" darkness and "put on" light.

46 The Epiphany is the feast that commemorates the revealing of Jesus as the Christ, the Son of God, beginning with the star that drew the Magi, the wise men, to come see the babe in Bethlehem. The remainder of the season after Epiphany focuses on other events in which we see glimpses of Christ's glory.

Created for the 1979 BCP, this particular prayer challenges us to be heralds of the Good News. The world will "perceive the glory of his marvelous works" as a result of our words and actions.

47 In the tenth chapter of John's Gospel, Jesus is described as the Good Shepherd who knows his sheep and calls them each by name. That passage, in turn, echoes Ezekiel 34 from the Hebrew scriptures, which speaks of God shepherding God's people.

Almighty God, give us grace to cast away the works of darkness, and put on the armor of light, now in the time of this mortal life in which your Son Jesus Christ came to visit us in great humility; that in the last day, when he shall come again in his glorious majesty to judge both the living and the dead, we may rise to the life immortal; through him who lives and reigns with you and the Holy Spirit, one God, now and for ever. Amen.[45]

CONTEMPORARY COLLECT FOR THE FIRST SUNDAY OF ADVENT

Give us grace, O Lord, to answer readily the call of our Savior Jesus Christ and proclaim to all people the Good News of his salvation, that we and the whole world may perceive the glory of his marvelous works; who lives and reigns with you and the Holy Spirit, one God, for ever and ever. Amen.[46]

CONTEMPORARY COLLECT FOR THE THIRD SUNDAY AFTER THE EPIPHANY

O God, whose Son Jesus is the good shepherd of your people: Grant that when we hear his voice we may know him who calls us each by name, and follow where he leads; who, with you and the Holy Spirit, lives and reigns, one God, for ever and ever. Amen.[47]

CONTEMPORARY COLLECT FOR THE FOURTH SUNDAY OF EASTER

❖ Pentecost (literally meaning "fiftieth day") is the Greek name for the Feast of Weeks, originally a Jewish feast associated with the giving of the Law on Mount Sinai to the people of Israel. As recorded in Acts 2, it was on that day that the Holy Spirit descended on Christ's apostles, so that they boldly proclaimed the Good News and saw three thousand added to their number. It is sometimes called Whitsunday, or "White Sunday," which can be confusing to some, as red is the color used for vestments and hangings in churches on that day. (Some believe that the white refers to the robes of those who were preparing to be baptized.)

The long period following Pentecost is called "Ordinary Time" in the Roman Catholic tradition, but in Episcopal churches and in the BCP it is referred to as the Season after Pentecost. Green is the color associated with this season, and the Gospel readings cover the public ministry of Christ preceding his Passion.

48 Reflecting on this collect, a wise bishop once got into the pulpit and simply said, "Love God, love each other." This is, as Jesus once told a lawyer who questioned him, the great commandment.

49 It is interesting that the Wednesday, Friday, and Saturday following the Sunday on which this collect is used have traditionally been the autumn "Ember Days," days associated with the ordained ministry. It is a reminder that all ministry is possible only because of the grace of God, not our own ability.

50 It is little surprise that this prayer was composed for the 1549 Prayer Book, since it reflects that Reformation era's focus on the Holy Scriptures as the foundation for our faith and Christian life. The call to "inwardly digest them" is a reminder that scripture is not cotton candy, some ephemeral fluff, but rather something to be chewed on, something to be heard, read, and learned.

O God, you have taught us to keep all your commandments by loving you and our neighbor: Grant us the grace
of your Holy Spirit, that we may be devoted to you with
our whole heart, and united to one another with pure affection; through Jesus Christ our Lord, who lives and reigns
with you and the Holy Spirit, one God, for ever and ever.
Amen.[48]

CONTEMPORARY PROPER 9, IN THE SEASON AFTER PENTECOST

O God, because without you we are not able to please you,
mercifully grant that your Holy Spirit may in all things
direct and rule our hearts; through Jesus Christ our Lord,
who lives and reigns with you and the Holy Spirit, one
God, now and for ever. Amen.[49]

CONTEMPORARY PROPER 19, IN THE SEASON AFTER PENTECOST

Blessed Lord, who caused all holy Scriptures to be written for our learning: Grant us so to hear them, read, mark,
learn and inwardly digest them, that we may embrace and
ever hold fast the blessed hope of everlasting life, which
you have given us in our Savior Jesus Christ; who lives and
reigns with you and the Holy Spirit, one God, for ever and
ever. Amen.[50]

CONTEMPORARY PROPER 28, IN THE SEASON AFTER PENTECOST

51 The Feast of All Saints is one of the seven primary feasts of the Christian Church. Pope Gregory IV first mentioned it in a letter dated 835 to Louis the Pious, the Holy Roman emperor. Some say that the custom of commemorating all the saints goes as far back as the time of Saint Chrysostom.

Following continental reformers, Cranmer did not include in the 1549 Prayer Book feasts associated with any saints except those mentioned in the Christian scriptures, as well as this one all-inclusive feast remembering all. This collect was composed for that 1549 book and uses Saint Paul's image of the Body of Christ to speak of the faithful. You can almost picture muscles and sinews knit together into one working body. To those in any generation who believe and hope against the odds, this prayer is a reminder of the "ineffable joys" that await us if we can only persevere like the saints before us.

52 Pope Saint Leo the Great is reported to have said once, "The Son of God became the Son of Man that the sons of men might become the sons of God."

53 This prayer, especially appropriate on Fridays in remembrance of Christ's Passion, is an adaptation of a prayer found in the 1959 *Daily Prayer* by Eric Milner-White and G. W. Briggs.

Almighty God, you have knit together your elect in one communion and fellowship in the mystical body of your Son Christ our Lord: Give us grace so to follow your blessed saints in all virtuous and godly living, that we may come to those ineffable joys that you have prepared for those who truly love you; through Jesus Christ our Lord, who with you and the Holy Spirit lives and reigns, one God in glory everlasting. Amen.[51]

CONTEMPORARY COLLECT FOR ALL SAINTS DAY

O God, who wonderfully created, and yet more wonderfully restored, the dignity of human nature: Grant that we may share the divine life of him who humbled himself to share our humanity, your Son Jesus Christ; who lives and reigns with you, in the unity of the Holy Spirit, one God, for ever and ever. Amen.[52]

CONTEMPORARY COLLECT OF THE INCARNATION

Almighty God, whose beloved Son willingly endured the agony and shame of the cross for our redemption: Give us courage to take up our cross and follow him; who lives and reigns with you and the Holy Spirit, one God, now and for ever. Amen.[53]

CONTEMPORARY COLLECT OF THE HOLY CROSS

❖ In his *Commentary on the American Prayer Book*, Marion J. Hatchett speaks of the reluctance on the part of William White, former chaplain to the Continental Congress and first presiding bishop of the new Episcopal Church, to mark the Fourth of July as a special day of commemoration in the American Prayer Book of 1789. White was trying to be sensitive to the many clergy who had tried to remain loyal to the mother country and to the Church of England. He did not want to antagonize them further.

Likewise, although the Continental Congress had authorized thanksgiving to be made for harvests in the fall, the specific commemoration in November of Thanksgiving Day would come much later. It was not until the 1928 BCP that both days were included as lesser feasts, and it was only with the 1979 book that both were recognized as major feasts.

In offering these prayers, we give thanks for this land we call home, while also always remembering that the nation, like us, is as yet far from perfect. It is hoped that through our prayers and through our lives, we may make this indeed a place of liberty, hope, and justice for all.

54 This revision of an early collect changed this line that made reference to a direct connection with those founding fathers, something not possible either for Americans whose ancestors were later arrivals to this land or for Native Americans. This prayer thus makes a point of noting that the nation's founders "lit the torch of freedom for nations then unborn," a more inclusive understanding of those who today call this land home.

55 This prayer follows those that have been used in the past to give thanks to God for harvests and challenges us to consider our role as stewards of the "great bounty" all around us.

Lord God Almighty, in whose Name the founders of this country won liberty for themselves and for us, and lit the torch of freedom for nations then unborn:[54] Grant that we and all the people of this land may have grace to maintain our liberties in righteousness and peace; through Jesus Christ our Lord, who lives and reigns with you and the Holy Spirit, one God for ever and ever. Amen.

CONTEMPORARY COLLECT FOR INDEPENDENCE DAY

Almighty and gracious Father, we give you thanks for the fruits of the earth in their season and for the labors of those who harvest them. Make us, we pray, faithful stewards of your great bounty, for the provision of our necessities and the relief of all who are in need, to the glory of your Name; through Jesus Christ our Lord, who lives and reigns with you and the Holy Spirit, one God, now and for ever. Amen.[55]

CONTEMPORARY COLLECT FOR THANKSGIVING DAY

2 □ Belonging and Building Relationships

If you are sitting in a pew in an Episcopal church and reach forward to pick up a Prayer Book in front of you, you will likely find that while most of the book's pages look pristine, one small section will be worn around the edges. This is because those pages, the 300s, contain the two services that engage the congregation the majority of the time that they use the book: Baptism and the Eucharist, the rites of initiation and communion.

Religious communities, like other human groups, have prescribed ways of welcoming in new members and shared experiences that help perpetuate their bonds of belonging. The Book of Common Prayer built on patterns inherited from the earliest days of Christianity, refining or revising them in each new edition. Certain basic elements have remained consistent from the start: baptizing initiates in water as a sign of rebirth, anointing with oil as a seal of the baptism, and including them in the ongoing communal meal of bread and wine.

Questions about timing of certain actions and specific procedures have abounded through the centuries: When is someone baptized, as an adult or an infant? When does the baptized member receive Communion for the first time? Is sprinkling or pouring as appropriate as full immersion? Should non-alcoholic juice be used instead of wine? Volumes have been written and immeasurable time and energy on the part of different traditions have been spent on these and similar questions.

But in the pages that follow, we will see that the Prayer Book is not meant to be an encyclopedia or technical blueprint. Those worn, familiar pages that are used week in and week out remain focused not on answering all the questions, but on experiencing the reality that we are one with God and with one another as brothers and sisters in Christ through water and the breaking of the bread.

❖ The service of Holy Baptism took on a newly rediscovered importance with the 1979 Prayer Book, with all the other sacramental rites arising from it. Although it is by definition a singular experience, it can be such a helpful thing to go back to the words of that service and learn once more from it.

1 The rubrics in the Prayer Book are the directions, not usually very exciting or inspiring. Yet these words from page 298 of the Prayer Book must rank among the most important, the most powerful in the book. "Full initiation," it says, a bond that is "indissoluble." For any believer who has ever doubted, for any Christian who has ever gone through a place of shadows, these words echo Saint Paul's promise that there is nothing that can separate us from the love of God (Romans 8:38–39).

2 These words from the opening of the baptismal service come from Ephesians 4:4–6, a reminder that we who are so diverse, so different from one another are united in Christ.

3 In the prayer over the baptismal font, the Prayer Book offers a brief summary of the meaning of water in the life of the people of God: from creation in the book of Genesis through the parting of the Red Sea to the baptism of Jesus in the river Jordan. It then moves to the meaning of the baptismal water for the believer: death and resurrection, rebirth, a new start, and incorporation into the family of God.

Holy Baptism is full initiation by water and the Holy Spirit into Christ's Body, the Church. The bond which God establishes in Baptism is indissoluble.[1]

There is one Body and one Spirit;
There is one hope in God's call to us;
One Lord, one Faith, one Baptism;
One God and Father of all.[2]

We thank you, Almighty God, for the gift of water. Over it the Holy Spirit moved in the beginning of creation. Through it you led the children of Israel out of their bondage in Egypt into the land of promise. In it your Son Jesus received the baptism of John and was anointed by the Holy Spirit as the Messiah, the Christ, to lead us, through his death and resurrection, from the bondage of sin into everlasting life.

We thank you, Father, for the water of Baptism. In it we are buried with Christ in his death. By it we share in his resurrection. Through it we are reborn by the Holy Spirit. Therefore in joyful obedience to your Son, we bring into his fellowship those who come to him in faith, baptizing them in the Name of the Father, and of the Son, and of the Holy Spirit.[3]

FROM THE SERVICE OF HOLY BAPTISM

❖ The Baptismal Covenant was new to the 1979 BCP and has become a central theme in the Episcopal Church. It combines creedal affirmations with promises for how to live. Belief leads to action. Faith in the Triune God, the Divine One who is accessible to the core, leads to a determination to live out that faith in relational ways with all those we encounter. In the words often attributed to Saint Francis of Assisi, "Preach the gospel at all times; if necessary, use words." Faith is about more than what we say we believe—it is also about what we show in and through our lives. The five questions presented are an expansion of the single question posed in the 1662 version: "Wilt thou then obediently keep God's holy will and commandments, and walk in the same all the days of thy life?"

4 Both the Nicene Creed, the statement of faith used in each Eucharistic service that dates back to the 300s, and the even earlier Apostles' Creed, owe their origins to the question and answer format of the earliest baptismal formularies. "Do you believe?" the baptismal candidate is asked. "I believe," she or he answers. That person does not answer alone. All Christians present are invited to join in renewing their faith. "I believe ... I believe."

5 The first of the five "action" questions is drawn directly out of the Acts of the Apostles 2:42, where the earliest believers were said to do these very things, signs of their common life in Christ.

6 The fifth and final question expands on the fourth, and indeed on all that Jesus taught about making a difference for "the least of these" (Matthew 25:40). The answer to this question and the four that preceded it is a bold "I will," but coupled with a reminder of the only way that we truly are able to do so, "with God's help."

Do you believe in God the Father?

Do you believe in Jesus Christ, the Son of God?

Do you believe in God the Holy Spirit?[4]

Will you continue in the apostles' teaching and fellowship, in the breaking of bread, and in the prayers?[5]

Will you persevere in resisting evil, and, whenever you fall into sin, repent and return to the Lord?

Will you proclaim by word and example the Good News of God in Christ?

Will you seek and serve Christ in all persons, loving your neighbor as yourself?

Will you strive for justice and peace among all people, and respect the dignity of every human being?[6]
I will, with God's help.

THE BAPTISMAL COVENANT, FROM THE SERVICE OF HOLY BAPTISM

❖ Baptism means belonging. At least, that is what the prayers following Baptism remind us. Even as the prayer over the water emphasized the death and resurrection aspects of the water of Baptism, so these prayers focus on incorporation into Christ's Body, into the family of God. We are adopted; we are God's children. We shall never be alone again.

7 This post-baptismal prayer has in times past been called the prayer for the sevenfold gifts of the Spirit. The idea is that, thanks to Baptism, the person is forgiven, but also sustained for the years to come.

8 How often I have returned to these words when I feel uncertain, anxious. These wonderful words come as the newly baptized person is sealed with oil on the forehead. The image, of course, is that of sheep who are marked so that all who see them will know that they do indeed belong. We are called to know who we are, but also *whose* we are, and not just for a time, but for ever.

9 This last prayer is used only when the Baptism is not followed imme-diately by a Eucharist. After the baptizing with water and the anointing with oil, the people of the congregation add their blessing, as it were, in these words of welcome to the newest member of their spiritual family. The entire worshipping community joins in a prayer of thanks-giving for making all of us "worthy to share in the inheritance of the saints in light."

Heavenly Father, we thank you that by water and the Holy
Spirit you have bestowed upon these your servants the
forgiveness of sin, and have raised them to the new life
of grace. Sustain them, O Lord, in your Holy Spirit. Give
them an inquiring and discerning heart, the courage to will
and to persevere, a spirit to know and to love you, and the
gift of joy and wonder in all your works. Amen.[7]

You are sealed by the Holy Spirit in Baptism and marked as
Christ's own for ever. Amen.[8]

We receive you into the household of God. Confess the
faith of Christ crucified, proclaim his resurrection, and
share with us in his eternal priesthood.

All praise and thanks to you, most merciful Father, for
adopting us as your own children, for incorporating us into
your holy Church, and for making us worthy to share in the
inheritance of the saints in light; through Jesus Christ your
Son our Lord, who lives and reigns with you and the Holy
Spirit, one God, for ever and ever. Amen.[9]

FROM THE SERVICE OF HOLY BAPTISM

❖ The Exhortation extends back before the 1549 BCP to the Order for Communion of 1548, where it was intended to serve as a tool for helping the people prepare their hearts to receive the sacrament. Far from being overly pessimistic in tone, the Exhortation actually places our need for repentance in the context of "God's great love for us." It is because we are so loved that we can dare to face our own failings and seek forgiveness.

This section of the Prayer Book is rarely used anymore and only found in the traditional-language Rite I, not Rite II. This is regrettable, as it can be a healthy and wonderful thing to take stock before we come to Communion, or indeed at the start of a new day, and remember that we always need to ask for mercy, but also that we have a God who loves us even before we ask.

10 People who read Saint Paul's epistles often speak of his penchant for long, run-on sentences. As we see here, Cranmer clearly shared this tendency. This paragraph is actually one lengthy sentence, but what a sentence it is! It begins with a reminder of God's great love for us and goes on to list the many reasons why—beyond obeying God's command—we should offer thanks. In many ways, it is a mini-creed and thus a reminder that our statements of faith are also statements of thanksgiving.

11 Here we see an explicit reminder of what is implied in every confession: true repentance requires a change in how we live from this point onward. As Jesus said to the woman caught in adultery in John's Gospel: "Neither do I condemn you. Go your way, and from now on do not sin again" (8:10).

12 This is a wonderful Old English way of speaking about our moral obligation, the "duty and service" that we are bound to give to God.

Having in mind, therefore, his great love for us, and in obedience to his command, his Church renders to Almighty God our heavenly Father never-ending thanks for the creation of the world, for his continual providence over us, for his love for all mankind, and for the redemption of the world by our Savior Christ, who took upon himself our flesh, and humbled himself even to death on the cross, that he might make us the children of God by the power of the Holy Spirit, and exalt us to everlasting life.[10]

Examine your lives and conduct by the rule of God's commandments, that you may perceive wherein you have offended in what you have done or left undone, whether in thought, word, or deed. And acknowledge your sins before Almighty God, with full purpose of amendment of life....[11]

To Christ our Lord who loves us, and washed us in his own blood, and made us a kingdom of priests to serve his God and Father, to him be glory in the Church evermore. Through him let us offer continually the sacrifice of praise, which is our bounden duty and service,[12] and, with faith in him, come boldly before the throne of grace [and humbly confess our sins to Almighty God].

THE EXHORTATION, FROM HOLY EUCHARIST I

❖ The Ten Commandments are, of course, foundational to the Judeo-Christian heritage, indeed to Western society as a whole. Yet it is remarkable how few people today can recite the whole Decalogue ("deca" = ten). This recital of the commandments in versicle-response fashion is used in Lent or at some other penitential time in the life of a congregation. Although the summary of the Law by Jesus ("Love God, love your neighbor") can be used instead, the Decalogue remains an important tool for helping us ask ourselves how we are doing.

When read in light of Jesus's further clarifications in the Sermon on the Mount, we might well ask ourselves if we have murdered someone in our hearts today, stolen someone's joy, lusted after another. Some choose to ignore all this because it can be depressing to face our own failings. But in truth it can be liberating to shine a light on things that we need to confess, even if only to God and ourselves, and then repent or turn away from them, thereby growing both as children of God and as more fully realized, redeemed human beings.

A particularly helpful exercise can be to follow a personal inventory using the "thou shalt not's" of the Ten Commandments with a more positive list such as is found in 1 Corinthians 13, the so-called love chapter. Replacing the words "love is" with "I will be," and ending with a reminder of where we find the grace to accomplish all that we promise, we can say:

"I will be patient. I will be kind. I will not be envious or boastful or arrogant. I will not insist on my own way. I will not be irritable or resentful. I will not rejoice in wrongdoing, but will rejoice in the truth. I will bear all things, believe all things, hope all things, endure all things. All this I will do with God's help."

Hear the commandments of God to his people:
I am the Lord your God who brought you out of bondage.
You shall have no other gods but me.
Amen. Lord have mercy.

You shall not make for yourself any idol.
Amen. Lord have mercy.

You shall not invoke with malice the Name of the Lord
your God.
Amen. Lord have mercy.

Remember the Sabbath Day and keep it holy.
Amen. Lord have mercy.

Honor your father and your mother.
Amen. Lord have mercy.

You shall not commit murder.
Amen. Lord have mercy.

You shall not commit adultery.
Amen. Lord have mercy.

You shall not steal.
Amen. Lord have mercy.

You shall not be a false witness.
Amen. Lord have mercy.

You shall not covet anything that belongs to your
neighbor.
Amen. Lord have mercy.

THE DECALOGUE, FROM THE PENITENTIAL ORDER RITE II

❖ Following the Exhortation and Decalogue is the Penitential Order, which includes a confession and absolution in traditional language. This particular form dates back to the 1552 BCP, although two particularly difficult lines were omitted in this Prayer Book, namely "and there is no health in us" and "miserable offenders." Still, this version retains the Reformation penitential themes and is filled with scripture and scriptural allusions. The key source text is the seventh chapter of Romans, where the apostle speaks at length of his sinfulness, but echoes of Isaiah 53, Psalm 51, Psalm 119, Titus 2, 1 Peter 2, 1 John 2, and other passages can be heard.

The opening lines recall Jesus's words about being the Good Shepherd who goes after his lost sheep, a reminder that in confessing our sinfulness to God, we are confessing to the One who is ready not only to forgive, but also to absolve, as if we had never sinned at all. This is the meaning of absolution and remission. It is like the passage from Isaiah 1:18 that declares, "Though your sins are like scarlet, they shall be like snow."

Almighty and most merciful Father,
We have erred and strayed from thy ways like lost sheep,
we have followed too much the devices and desires of our
own hearts,
we have offended against thy holy laws,
we have left undone those things which we ought to have
done,
and we have done those things which we ought not to have
done.
But thou, O Lord, have mercy upon us,
spare thou those who confess their faults,
restore thou those who are penitent,
according to thy promises declared unto mankind
in Christ Jesus our Lord.
And grant, O most merciful Father, for his sake, that we
may hereafter live a godly, righteous, and sober life,
to the glory of thy holy Name. Amen.

The Almighty and merciful Lord grant you absolution and
remission of all your sins, true repentance, amendment of
life, and the grace and consolation of his Holy Spirit. Amen.

THE CONFESSION AND ABSOLUTION,
FROM THE PENITENTIAL ORDER RITE I

13 Beginning with the 1549 Prayer Book, it became customary after hearing scripture read, a sermon preached, and the creed professed to take a moment to pray, not only for ourselves, but also for the entire church. Four centuries later, the form of this important prayer has remained very much the same, although now the first line makes it clear that we pray not only for the church, but also for the entire world in which we live. Such an expansive opening shows that we are called with hearts open to the needs of all, and trust in God who made all.

14 The first two paragraphs focus on the church and its ordained ministers and contain special concern for its "spirit of truth, unity, and concord." To "live in unity and godly love" is perhaps the greatest example of God at work.

15 This prayer makes clear that it is not just ordained people who make a difference. Far from it! While the old language of "meek heart and due reverence" may seem a bit passive in the twenty-first century, it is significant that the Prayer Book is clear about how grace-filled laypeople can serve God, and most likely in ways that priests and bishops never could, inasmuch as they are actually out there, side by side with their neighbors and co-workers.

Let us pray for the whole state of Christ's Church and the world.[13]

Almighty and everliving God, who in thy holy Word has taught us to make prayers, and supplications, and to give thanks for all men: Receive these our prayers which we offer unto thy divine Majesty, beseeching thee to inspire continually the Universal Church with the spirit of truth, unity, and concord; and grant that all those who do confess thy holy Name may agree in the truth of thy holy Word, and live in unity and godly love.

Give grace, O heavenly Father, to all bishops and other ministers, that they may, both by their life and doctrine, set forth thy true and lively Word, and rightly and duly administer thy holy Sacraments.[14]

And to all thy people give thy heavenly grace, and especially to this congregation here present; that, with meek heart and due reverence, they may hear and receive thy holy Word, truly serving thee in holiness and righteousness all the days of their life.[15]

THE PRAYERS OF THE PEOPLE, FROM HOLY EUCHARIST RITE I

16 The relationship of persons of faith to political authorities has always been a sensitive issue. Stories abound in the Hebrew scriptures of prophets sometimes honoring and sometimes challenging rulers. Just consider the complex relationship of the prophet Nathan with King David, especially after the affair with Bathsheba. Later, the response Jesus gave to the question about whether it was appropriate to pay taxes to the Roman government—"Give to the emperor the things that are the emperor's, and to God the things that are God's" (Mark 12:17)—were challenging not only to his listeners then but to his followers ever since. Another difficult passage is Romans 13:1, in which Saint Paul told the Christians in Rome that it was their duty to honor civil authorities.

From the first BCP of 1549, prayers were included for the English monarch, and the practice continued, albeit modified for the new context, in the church in America. Note that in this latest version of the Prayer Book, the prayer is expanded to include authorities in other lands as well.

17 This is the one section of the Prayers of the People new to the 1979 BCP, reflecting a concern for our stewardship of the earth.

18 Prayers for the deceased were commonplace in medieval times, as the concept of Purgatory, where souls underwent pain and purging before they could be allowed entrance into Paradise, resulted in Christians praying on behalf of their loved ones in an effort to decrease their time of torment. Reformation leaders did away with these practices, and prayers for the dead were not included in early versions of the BCP. It was in the 1928 BCP that the current petition was added, a controversial move at the time. It offers a view of growth in love and service in God's Kingdom.

We beseech thee also so to rule the hearts of those who bear the authority of government in this and every land, that they may be led to wise decisions and right actions for the welfare and peace of the world.[16]

Open, O Lord, the eyes of all people to behold thy gracious hand in all thy works, that, rejoicing in thy whole creation, they may honor thee with their substance, and be faithful stewards of thy bounty.[17]

And we most humbly beseech thee of thy goodness, O Lord, to comfort and succor all those who, in this transitory life, are in trouble, sorrow, need, sickness, or any other adversity.

And we also bless thy holy Name for all thy servants departed this life in thy faith and fear, beseeching thee to grant them continual growth in thy love and service; and to grant us grace so to follow the good examples of all thy saints, that with them we may be partakers of thy heavenly Kingdom.[18]

Grant these our prayers, O Father, for Jesus Christ's sake, our only mediator and advocate. Amen.

THE PRAYERS OF THE PEOPLE FROM HOLY EUCHARIST RITE I

❖ At the heart of the weekly worship service in the Episcopal or Anglican tradition (as well as the Roman Catholic, Orthodox, Lutheran, and other liturgically focused Christian traditions) is the Holy Eucharist, and at the heart of the Eucharist is the Great Thanksgiving, the Eucharistic Prayer. It is a retelling—no, a reliving—of Jesus's Last Supper with his apostles, in which followers of Christ today partake of his Body and Blood.

Eucharistic Prayer I of Rite I (the traditional-language service) hearkens back to the service in the first American Prayer Book of 1789, which itself incorporated the body of the service from the 1662 English BCP along with some additions from the Scottish service. The Great Thanksgiving is about our communion with God and one another. Having been instructed in God's holy Word, we share the family meal and gain strength for the spiritual journey.

19 Jesus died for us. It is such a simple, basic statement and yet it carries a message of the remarkable love of God, who not only created you and me, but also chose to redeem us from our own hurtful choices and failings. What happened on the cross was not just the death of a martyr for a cause—there have been countless martyrs who have died for many causes throughout the centuries—but rather it is "a full, perfect, and sufficient sacrifice, oblation, and satisfaction for the sins of the whole world." Here we see John 3:16, "For God so loved the world ..." spelled out in full, a reminder of what it cost God to redeem us.

20 The Institution Narrative is a conflation of scriptural texts about Jesus's words at the Last Supper, as he celebrated the Jewish Passover feast with his friends and gave it new meaning, telling them, and now us, each time that we partake of the sacrament, that "this is his Body, this is his Blood," given for us. See Mark 26:26–29.

All glory be to thee, Almighty God, our heavenly Father, for that thou, of thy tender mercy, didst give thine only Son Jesus Christ to suffer death upon the cross for our redemption; who made there, by his one oblation of himself once offered, a full, perfect, and sufficient sacrifice, oblation, and satisfaction, for the sins of the whole world; and did institute, and in his holy Gospel command us to continue, a perpetual memory of that his precious death and sacrifice, until his coming again.[19]

For in the night in which he was betrayed, he took bread; and when he had given thanks, he brake it, and gave it to his disciples, saying, "Take, eat, this is my Body, which is given for you. Do this in remembrance of me."

Likewise, after supper, he took the cup; and when he had given thanks, he gave it to them, saying, "Drink ye all of this; for this is my Blood of the New Testament, which is shed for you, and for many, for the remission of sins. Do this, as oft as ye shall drink it, in remembrance of me."[20]

THE GREAT THANKSGIVING, FROM HOLY EUCHARIST RITE I

❖ The Great Thanksgiving in Holy Eucharist II consists of four Eucharistic prayers, each one similar to the other, but each one emphasizing slightly different themes.

Prayer A is the one most commonly used in Episcopal churches and focuses on humankind's fall from grace and the resulting flawed human condition.

Prayer B, often used in the season of Advent leading up to Christmas, emphasizes the incarnation, the coming of Christ into the world.

21 "Infinite love"—what wonderful words! What a glorious way of understanding ourselves and our place in the heart of the Creator. As has been wisely said, God as God could not save humanity, but God as human being—sharing our human nature, living and dying as one of us—could, and did.

22 The beautiful lyrical quality of this prayer makes it a wonderful treasure to use any time in one's personal devotional life. With every recital, we are reminded that in Christ, we have been delivered from evil, made worthy to stand before God, brought out of error, sin, and death into truth and righteousness and life. It is the Good News of the Christian faith wrapped up in poetic form.

Holy and gracious Father: In your infinite love[21] you made us for yourself; and, when we had fallen into sin and become subject to evil and death, you, in your mercy, sent Jesus Christ, your only and eternal Son, to share our human nature, to live and die as one of us, to reconcile us to you, the God and Father of all.

He stretched out his arms upon the cross, and offered himself, in obedience to your will, a perfect sacrifice for the whole world.

FROM HOLY EUCHARIST RITE II, EUCHARISTIC PRAYER A

We give thanks to you, O God, for the goodness and love which you have made known to us in creation; in the calling of Israel to be your people; in your Word spoken through the prophets; and above all in the Word made flesh, Jesus, your Son. For in these last days you sent him to be incarnate from the Virgin Mary, to be the Savior and Redeemer of the world. In him, you have delivered us from evil, and made us worthy to stand before you. In him, you have brought us out of error into truth, out of sin into righteousness, out of death into life.[22]

FROM HOLY EUCHARIST RITE II, EUCHARISTIC PRAYER B

❖ Eucharistic Prayer C is the most interactive with its many responses throughout the prayer. It stresses the ongoing revelation of God to us, through nature, through the prophets, and ultimately through Christ.

23 Here we see the ancient creation narrative of Genesis merged with modern scientific understandings of the vastness of the universe, culminating with a marvelous image of the planet on which we live, "this fragile earth, our island home." Hardly the center of the universe as some medieval thinkers believed, we are instead floating along on our tiny island in the vast cosmos. Far from insignificant, we, like all of creation, are in the hands of a loving God.

24 There's no debate here between creation and evolution, but rather the recognition that we were created from the "primal elements." But it is still God who did the creating.

God of all power, Ruler of the Universe, you are worthy of glory and praise.
Glory to you for ever and ever.

At your command all things came to be: the vast expanse of interstellar space, galaxies, suns, the planets in their courses, and this fragile earth, our island home.[23]
By your will they were created and have their being.

From the primal elements you brought forth the human race,[24] and blessed us with memory, reason, and skill. You made us the rulers of creation. But we turned against you, and betrayed your trust; and we turned against one another.
Have mercy, Lord, for we are sinners in your sight.

Again and again, you called us to return. Through prophets and sages you revealed your righteous Law. And in the fullness of time you sent your only Son, born of a woman, to fulfill your Law, to open for us the way of freedom and peace.
By his blood, he reconciled us.
By his wounds, we are healed.

FROM HOLY EUCHARIST RITE II, PRAYER C

❖ Eucharistic Prayer D is the lengthiest prayer and used more during the penitential season of Lent. It finds its origins in the prayer of Saint Basil in the fourth century. In the ecumenical spirit that was prevalent in the 1970s, it was adopted by many of the major Christian bodies, including the Roman Catholic, Orthodox, and Anglican churches, as a truly common prayer between them. It is the same spirit that led to the creation of the Revised Common Lectionary, which differs at times from the lectionary in the back of the Prayer Book. It is the lectionary now used by the Episcopal Church and will be printed in future editions of the 1979 BCP.

25 Here we see the balance of what it means to be stewards of creation, to "rule and serve" all God's creatures. The world is in our care, but this does not mean that we can do whatever we want with it. Far from it. It means that we are accountable for it, accountable to God, to our children, and to our children's children.

26 What a beautiful combination of two verses of scripture. "For God so loved the world" from John 3:16 intermixes here with "when the fullness of time had come, God sent his Son" from Galatians 4:4.

27 A paraphrase of Isaiah 61, we hear the purpose of Christ's coming: to bring life and hope to those who need both. That purpose included death on the cross, but thankfully it also included resurrection and new life, not only for Christ, and not even just for all of us, but for all of creation.

We acclaim you, holy Lord, glorious in power. Your mighty works reveal your wisdom and love. You formed us in your own image, giving the whole world into our care, so that, in obedience to you, our Creator, we might rule and serve all your creatures.[25] When our disobedience took us far from you, you did not abandon us to the power of death. In your mercy you came to our help, so that in seeking you we might find you. Again and again you called us into covenant with you, and through the prophets you taught us to hope for salvation.

Father, you loved the world so much that in the fullness of time you sent your only Son to be our Savior.[26] Incarnate by the Holy Spirit, born of the Virgin Mary, he lived as one of us, yet without sin. To the poor he proclaimed the good news of salvation; to prisoners, freedom; to the sorrowful, joy. To fulfill your purpose he gave himself up to death; and, rising from the grave, destroyed death, and made the whole creation new.[27]

And, that we might live no longer for ourselves, but for him who died and rose for us, he sent the Holy Spirit, his own first gift for those who believe, to complete his work in the world, and to bring to fulfillment the sanctification of all.

From Eucharist Rite II, Eucharistic Prayer D

❖ It is a delicate balance to recognize our intrinsic value, to claim our heritage as beloved children of God, and at the same time to admit that we are not worthy of so much good that may come to us. This is not simply a religious proposition, but a human reality. We are infinitely special and seriously flawed. We are living icons, beautiful images of God in the world, but the icons are marred, scarred, imperfect. This prayer is not intended to make us depressed, but to remind us that it is never helpful to presume that it is our right to be loved by God and others. It is not our right; it is a gift. It is grace.

28 This line comes from one of the most controversial passages in the Gospel narratives, namely the story in Mark 7:24–30, of Jesus and the Syro-Phoenician woman. In the story, which is not found in the other three canonical Gospels, a foreign woman comes to Jesus and begs him to heal her daughter. Jesus's response is one that has confused, and even angered, readers ever since. "It is not fair to take the children's food and throw it to the dogs" (Mark 7:27). Her reply reveals both her shrewdness and her tenacity: "Sir, even the dogs under the table eat the children's crumbs" (Mark 7:28). Impressed with her response, Jesus commends her faith and grants her request. But his initial words are still curious and have resulted in many different interpretations of the conundrum of that text.

29 The Prayer of Humble Access is not included in Rite II, the service in contemporary language, but only found in Rite I, reflecting its history in the older versions of the Prayer Book.

We do not presume to come to this thy Table, O merciful Lord, trusting in our own righteousness, but in thy manifold and great mercies. We are not worthy so much as to gather up the crumbs under thy Table.[28] But thou art the same Lord whose property is always to have mercy. Grant us therefore, gracious Lord, so to eat the flesh of thy dear Son Jesus Christ, and to drink his blood, that we may evermore dwell in him, and he in us. Amen.

PRAYER OF HUMBLE ACCESS,[29] FROM HOLY EUCHARIST RITE I

❖ It is the most familiar prayer for Christians the world over. It is first found in the Gospels, when the disciples came to Jesus and asked him to teach them how to pray, just as other famous rabbis would instruct their followers in the ways of prayer. Jesus's reply was brief and simple, yet incredibly profound.

The prayer opens with praise to a holy God who at the same time is a loving parent to us. It goes on to express hope that the divine purpose that is a reality in paradise would also be realized here in our world, and it makes the request that God would give us what we need to make it through today, even as God once gave manna to the Israelites during their wanderings in the wilderness, just enough to get them through each day. It speaks of being forgiven for our sins even as we forgive those who hurt us. It begs for divine help to get us through times of trial and rescue us from the darkness in which we find ourselves, and then concludes with the recognition that God's reign and power are greater than all the forces we could ever face.

It is the Lord's Prayer. It is the church's prayer. It is the prayer of every individual who lifts her or his eyes upward in desperate hope, daring to trust in the God and Father who loves us.

Our Father in heaven,
  hallowed be your Name,
  your kingdom come,
  your will be done,
  on earth as in heaven.
Give us today our daily bread.
Forgive us our sins
  as we forgive those
  who sin against us.
Save us from the time of trial,
  and deliver us from evil.
For the kingdom, the power,
  and the glory are yours,
  now and for ever. Amen.

THE LORD'S PRAYER, CONTEMPORARY VERSION

❖ Having received the bread and wine, the Body and Blood of Christ, and having participated in the family meal, the congregation offers one last prayer before being sent forth into the world. It is a prayer of thanks and an acceptance of our mission, which is only possible with the "strength and courage" that God alone can give. The bishop or priest responds with the pronouncement of God's blessing, an affirmation of our commissioning as apostles (literally "sent ones") who can now go into the world to "love and serve." We have been instructed, we have been forgiven, we have been spiritually fed, we have been blessed ... and now we are sent forth. No wonder our departing words are, "Thanks be to God."

Eternal God, heavenly Father,
You have graciously accepted us as living members
of your Son our Savior Jesus Christ,
and you have fed us with spiritual food
in the Sacrament of his Body and Blood.
Send us now into the world in peace,
and grant us strength and courage to love and serve you
with gladness and singleness of heart;
through Christ our Lord. Amen.

POST-COMMUNION PRAYER, FROM THE HOLY EUCHARIST RITE II

❖ Ash Wednesday did not receive its name until the ninth century, when the imposition of ashes as a sign of both mortality and repentance was added to a much older penitential service designed as the starting point of the forty-day season of Lent, leading up to Easter.

As is probably fairly obvious by this point, the Prayer Book in all its various versions has been forthright about addressing the plain fact of our individual and corporate sinfulness. While some dismiss this as negativism, the fact is that we humans, whatever our faith or philosophy, spend a lot of time hiding our failings from others and even from ourselves. We sweep them under the carpet, ignore or excuse them, sidestep any admission that we might actually have done or said hurtful things.

These words of exhortation, adapted from the Canadian Prayer Book, remind us what a gift it can be to own up to what we have done and failed to do, and find sweet release from the weight of our continual efforts to hide behind some kind of veneer of goodness. The ashes placed on our forehead are not some badge of honor to give us further reason to boast (just another form of denial). Rather they are a powerful statement that our time on this earth is limited, so we can't afford to wait to repent. Now is the time to quit playing the game, take off the various masks we hide behind, and let God make us truly a new creation.

30 The first part of this exhortation offers a brief review of the history of Lent and its various aspects, while the subsequent invitation to the observance of a holy Lent includes several aspects of a spiritually healthy, holistic life, including fasting and self-denial as well as prayer and self-examination.

31 The words for the imposition of ashes call to mind Genesis 3:19 and the curse on Adam after his sin in Eden.

Dear People of God: The first Christians observed with great devotion the days of our Lord's passion and resurrection, and it became the custom of the Church to prepare for them by a season of penitence and fasting. This season of Lent provided a time in which converts to the faith were prepared for Holy Baptism. It was also a time when those who, because of notorious sins, had been separated from the body of the faithful were reconciled by penitence and forgiveness, and restored to the fellowship of the Church. Thereby, the whole congregation was put in mind of the message of pardon and absolution set forth in the Gospel of our Savior, and of the need which all Christians continually have to renew their repentance and faith.[30]

I invite you, therefore, in the name of the Church, to the observance of a holy Lent, by self-examination and repentance; by prayer, fasting, and self-denial; and by reading and meditating on God's holy Word. And, to make a right beginning of repentance, and as a mark of our mortal nature, let us now kneel before the Lord, our maker and redeemer.

Remember that you are dust and to dust you shall return.[31]

THE EXHORTATION, FROM THE ASH WEDNESDAY SERVICE

❖ In this litany we find a checklist, as it were, of specific ways in which we hurt others, ourselves, and God. As such, this can be a most helpful tool not only on Ash Wednesday, but any time that we want to consider the specifics of our failings rather than make some vague, easily dismissed confession. It is one thing to say, "I've sinned," and quite another to admit the very specific ways we have done so. To belong to God's family means looking at how our specific words and actions really do either strengthen or weaken the bonds between us all. The gift of Ash Wednesday and the forty days of Lent is that it can be a time of intentional reconnection, between God and us, and between our sisters and brothers and us.

To make the most of this prayer, it can be helpful to ask "how" I have been "self-indulgent" or "[exploited] other people" or "[envied] those more fortunate than myself." Twelve-step programs have long recognized the value of writing down specific wrongs done against others and then finding ways to make amends. The result is a healthier person who can begin to know inner peace.

This litany can be a wonderful help in that process. "We confess to you, Lord. Accept our repentance."

We confess to you, Lord, all our past unfaithfulness: the pride, hypocrisy, and impatience of our lives,
We confess to you, Lord.

Our self-indulgent appetites and ways, and our exploitation of other people,
We confess to you, Lord.

Our anger at our own frustration, and our envy of those more fortunate than ourselves,
We confess to you, Lord.

Our intemperate love of worldly goods and comforts, and our dishonesty in daily life and work,
We confess to you, Lord.

Our negligence in prayer and worship, and our failure to commend the faith that is in us,
We confess to you, Lord.

Accept our repentance, Lord, for the wrongs we have done: for our blindness to human need and suffering, and our indifference to injustice and cruelty,
Accept our repentance, Lord.

For all false judgments, for uncharitable thoughts toward our neighbors, and for our prejudice and contempt toward those who differ from us,
Accept our repentance, Lord.

FROM THE ASH WEDNESDAY SERVICE

❖ Palm Sunday has long served as the starting point of a week so special in the church year that it is appropriately called Holy Week. It is the week in which we commemorate the last days of Jesus leading up to and including his betrayal and death by crucifixion, and ultimately, his resurrection on Easter morning.

As such, Palm Sunday is a kind of bridge day, beginning with a celebration of the triumphal entry of Jesus into Jerusalem, when the crowds were so excited that they laid palm branches down on the ground before him, like an ancient red-carpet entrance fit for the "Son of David," the anticipated Messiah, the King of Israel. Congregations often begin the service outside, singing hymns, hearing the Gospel story of that famous entry into the holy city, and then processing in with the clergy and choir singing praises to God, just as the crowds did two thousand years ago.

Then, the mood begins to darken, as we hear the reading of the Passion Gospel, often in dramatic form with different readers taking the part of Jesus, Peter, Pontius Pilate, and the rest of the characters in the story. There is often no sermon this day, as the Gospel reading says everything that needs to be said, culminating with the burial of Jesus. It is a preview of the week to come, sober and solemn, and the final hymn is nothing less than a dirge, far different from the song of praise that opened the service.

In this one service, we move from joy and celebration to pain and suffering. It is a reminder that Jesus, the Divine Lover of our souls, has joined us in the human journey, has walked with us through the valley of the shadow of death, has endured the dark night of the soul and the agony of abandonment. Whatever you and I are going through, we can take some comfort from Holy Week. For in our deepest struggles, we are never alone.

Blessed is the King who comes in the name of the Lord.
Peace in heaven and glory in the highest.

It is right to praise you, Almighty God, for the acts of love
by which you have redeemed us through your Son Jesus
Christ our Lord. On this day he entered the holy city of
Jerusalem in triumph, and was proclaimed as King of kings
by those who spread their garments and branches of palm
along his way. Let these branches be for us signs of his victory, and grant that we who bear them in his name may
ever hail him as our King, and follow him in the way that
leads to eternal life; who lives and reigns in glory with you
and the Holy Spirit, now and for ever. Amen.

Blessed is he who comes in the name of the Lord.
Hosanna in the highest.

Almighty God, whose most dear Son went not up to joy
but first he suffered pain, and entered not into glory before
he was crucified: Mercifully grant that we, walking in the
way of the cross, may find it none other than the way of life
and peace; through Jesus Christ our Lord. Amen.

FROM THE PALM SUNDAY SERVICE

❖ The Maundy Thursday service, held in the evening , begins the Paschal Triduum or Holy Triduum—the three days—which continues through Easter Sunday. It is what Palm Sunday and the rest of Holy Week have led up to, indeed what all the church year has led up to. In medieval times, these final days of Holy Week were the culmination of a period of preparation for those who were about to be baptized at the Great Vigil of Easter. Likewise, those penitents who had been separated from the church because of notorious sins prepared for restoration at Easter.

Today, all Christian people can use these days as an important period of reflection on Christ's sacrifice of love for the world. Like Passover, from which it came, Maundy Thursday is the ultimate family time. In this one evening we find love, friendship, service, prayer, aloneness, foreboding, and a peace that passes understanding. It is the calm before the storm.

32 Many churches have instituted a foot-washing ceremony during their service that Thursday, echoing the example of Jesus at the Last Supper, as recorded in John 13:12–15. In the days of Jesus, weary travelers arriving at a home for dinner would often have their bare feet washed and anointed by a house servant. Jesus shocked his disciples by taking the role of a servant and doing the washing. As Mark 10:45 says, "For the Son of Man came not to be served, but to serve, and to give his life a ransom for many."

33 These comforting words come from John 14:27.

34 Here we find the meaning behind the designation "Maundy Thursday." It is so called because of the "mandate" or commandment that Jesus gave to his disciples in John 13:34–35, that they should love one another as he loved them.

Almighty Father, whose dear Son, on the night before he suffered, instituted the Sacrament of his Body and Blood: Mercifully grant that we may receive it thankfully in remembrance of Jesus Christ our Lord, who in these holy mysteries gives us a pledge of eternal life; and who now lives and reigns with you and the Holy Spirit, one God, for ever and ever. Amen.

The Lord Jesus, after he had supped with his disciples and had washed their feet, said to them, "Do you know what I, your Lord and Master, have done to you? I have given you an example, that you should do as I have done."[32]

Peace is my last gift to you, my own peace I now leave with you; peace which the world cannot give, I give to you.[33]

I give you a new commandment: Love one another as I have loved you.

By this shall the world know that you are my disciples: That you have love for one another.[34]

FROM THE MAUNDY THURSDAY SERVICE

❖ Everybody loves Easter Sunday, with its colorful eggs and joyful music and smiling faces. But the truth is that we really understand and relate more to Good Friday. For Easter is about victory, triumph, having arrived through the valley of the shadow of death. But for all of us still on this side of paradise, we have most certainly not yet arrived. Victory is something we have tasted only in small morsels. Easter is indeed our hope and our inheritance, but Good Friday is our more familiar companion.

In churches, this day is recognized through a service that includes the Solemn Collects, a lengthy set of prayers for all the world, and sometimes with a focus on the so-called seven last words of Christ, which conflates different quotes from the different Gospel accounts of the death of Jesus. The Eucharist is not celebrated on this day, or on the following day, Holy Saturday, in recognition of Jesus's death and burial in the tomb. However, many churches do offer Communion from the reserved Sacrament, the bread and wine consecrated the night before during the Maundy Thursday service.

35 This is perhaps the most explicit reference to the church as God's family. There is no denying that we are often a dysfunctional family, with more than a few problems and conflicts, but we can take comfort that Christ "was willing" to go through all that he did for this beloved family.

36 The image here is that of a redemptive shield or buffer between a flawed humankind and the divine judgment that we deserve.

37 Services on Holy Saturday, in recognition of Jesus's burial, are very brief and bare in form. It is a day of waiting, of keeping vigil.

Almighty God, we pray you graciously to behold this your family,[35] for whom our Lord Jesus Christ was willing to be betrayed, and given into the hands of sinners, and to suffer death upon the cross; who now lives and reigns with you and the Holy Spirit, one God, for ever and ever. Amen.

Lord Jesus Christ, Son of the living God, we pray you to set your passion, cross, and death between your judgment and our souls, now and in the hour of our death.[36] Give mercy and grace to the living; pardon and rest to the dead, to your holy Church peace and concord; and to us sinners everlasting life and glory; for with the Father and Holy Spirit you live and reign, one God, now and for ever. Amen.

FROM THE GOOD FRIDAY SERVICE

O God, Creator of heaven and earth: Grant that, as the crucified body of your dear Son was laid in the tomb and rested on this holy Sabbath,[37] so we may await with him the coming of the third day, and rise with him to newness of life; who now lives and reigns with you and the Holy Spirit, one God, for ever and ever. Amen.

FROM THE HOLY SATURDAY SERVICE

❖ The Great Vigil of Easter is our time to proclaim in a loud voice "Alleluia! Christ is Risen!" for in Christ's triumph over sin and death, our hopes are finally realized and our place at the banquet table is assured. It is the ultimate family reunion, beginning with a service of light, continuing with a series of scripture readings and prayers that take us through salvation history, and culminating with the initiating of new members of the Christian family through Baptism and the Holy Eucharist.

So central is the Easter message to Christianity that Saint Paul in 1 Corinthians 15:14 asserted that without the resurrection, our "faith has been in vain." During the darkest periods in our lives, we can take courage that we know the end of the story. Good wins. Evil is defeated. Life has the last word. "Death," as Paul goes on to say, "is swallowed up in victory" (1 Corinthians 15:54).

Thanks be to God! Alleluia, alleluia, alleluia!

38 The Exsultet, the great song of praise that opens the Easter Vigil, takes place between sunset on Holy Saturday and the rising of the sun on Easter morning. It is sung by a deacon or layperson and is accompanied by the lighting of the great Paschal Candle and smaller candles held by all those present in the congregation.

"This is the night," the song proclaims, and goes on in a series of triads to speak of the marvelous ways in which God has brought about redemption in the midst of darkness.

39 This is one of those great poetic moments in the BCP, with a beautiful image of a sinful humanity and a sinless God, seemingly irrevocably separated, ultimately reconciled on this blessed night. It is important to note that the 1979 BCP, while using contemporary English, at times did not use inclusive language, hence "man" here instead of "humankind." More recent liturgical works, such as *Enriching Our Worship*, intentionally use non-sexist language.

This is the night,[38] when you brought our fathers, the children of Israel, out of bondage in Egypt, and led them through the Red Sea on dry land.

This is the night, when all who believe in Christ are delivered from the gloom of sin, and are restored to grace and holiness of life.

This is the night, when Christ broke the bonds of death and hell, and rose victorious from the grave.

How wonderful and beyond our knowing, O God, is your mercy and loving-kindness to us, that to redeem a slave, you gave a Son.

How holy is this night, when wickedness is put to flight, and sin is washed away. It restores innocence to the fallen, and joy to those who mourn.
It casts out pride and hatred, and brings peace and concord.

How blessed is this night, when earth and heaven are joined and man is reconciled to God.[39]

THE EXSULTET, FROM THE EASTER VIGIL SERVICE

40 This rubric, or instruction on the service, explains the purpose of Confirmation as a sacramental act. As noted already, with the 1979 BCP, Holy Baptism took on a primary role as *the* rite of full initiation into the Body of Christ. No longer would Confirmation be seen as the completion of the baptismal act. No longer would children have to wait until they were confirmed as a rite of passage in order to receive Communion.

The rubrics here make clear that Confirmation is instead about making "a mature public affirmation of faith and commitment to the responsibilities of Baptism." To this end, the bishop, as the chief pastor of the local diocese and the representative of the church universal, lays hands on the heads of those being confirmed, asking God to strengthen them for service.

41 When a baptized Christian has already made a mature public affirmation of faith in another non-Anglican tradition, this is honored by not requiring that person to be re-confirmed. Rather she or he is formally received by the bishop, taking the person's hand and saying these words of recognition and welcome.

42 Confirmation, like Baptism, is viewed by Episcopalians and Anglicans as a non-repeated, one-time event. But there are times in one's spiritual journey when it is helpful to renew that Christian commitment, and for this reason the 1979 Prayer Book allows for such a reaffirmation.

43 This concluding prayer acknowledges the Holy Spirit's ongoing presence in the lives of those who have committed themselves to God in faith.

In the course of their Christian development, those baptized at an early age are expected, when they are ready and have been duly prepared, to make a mature public affirmation of their faith and commitment to the responsibilities of their Baptism and to receive the laying on of hands by the bishop.[40]

[For Confirmation] Strengthen, O Lord, your servant with your Holy Spirit; empower him for your service; and sustain him all the days of his life. Amen.

[For Reception] We recognize you as a member of the one, holy, catholic and apostolic Church, and we receive you into the fellowship of this Communion. God, the Father, Son, and Holy Spirit, bless, preserve, and keep you. Amen.[41]

[For Reaffirmation] May the Holy Spirit, who has begun a good work in you, direct and uphold you in the service of Christ and his kingdom. Amen.[42]

Almighty and everliving God, let your fatherly hand ever be over these your servants; let your Holy Spirit ever be with them; and so lead them in the knowledge and obedience of your Word, that they may serve you in this life, and dwell with you in the life to come; through Jesus Christ our Lord. Amen.[43]

FROM THE CONFIRMATION SERVICE

❖ To prepare baptized persons who have been away from the life of the church for a long time, and for those coming from other non-Anglican traditions, these questions are put to them during a Sunday Eucharist in front of the congregation. They intentionally presage the questions of the Baptismal Covenant that will be asked later when the persons are presented to the bishop for reception or reaffirmation.

In many ways, however, these questions are worth asking ourselves anytime, as we take stock of our own commitment to Christ and participation in the life of the Body of Christ.

44 As Christians, what more can we seek at any time than renewal of our life in Christ! As the next question points out, renewal involves going back to the promises we made, or that were made for us, at our own Baptism and considering how we are living into those promises now.

45 Some theologians have spoken of God's "preferential treatment of the poor." In other words, God loves everyone but has a special heart for those who seem to be the underdogs in life. We who seek to serve God must similarly have that same heart and find ways to make a difference in the lives of those who are powerless.

46 Here we see that God has given us gifts for a reason, to help usher in the Kingdom of God in our own world. There are echoes here of the Sermon on the Mount and, in particular, the Beatitudes. How blessed we and all the world would be if we chose to live a life counter-cultural to that which is all around us.

What do you seek?
Renewal of my life in Christ.[44]

In baptism, you died with Christ Jesus to the forces of evil
and rose to new life as members of his Body. Will you study
the promises made at your Baptism, and strive to keep them
in the fellowship of this community and the rest of the
Church?
I will, with God's help.

Will you attend the worship of God regularly with us, to
hear God's Word and to celebrate the mystery of Christ's
dying and rising?
I will, with God's help.

Will you participate in a life of service to those who are
poor, outcast, or powerless?[45]
I will, with God's help.

Will you strive to recognize the gifts that God has given
you and discern how they are to be used in the building up
of God's reign of peace and justice?[46]
I will, with God's help.

PREPARATION FOR REAFFIRMATION OF THE BAPTISMAL COVENANT,
IN THE BOOK OF OCCASIONAL SERVICES

3 □ Blessing in Times of Joy and Pain

God is with us when we laugh and when we weep. This is the principle behind the collection of services that follow the more familiar rites for Holy Baptism and the Eucharist. They are called Pastoral Services because they deal with crucial events in people's lives: marriage, the birth or adoption of a child, sickness, death. The prayers and proclamations found herein are among some of the most well known in the Prayer Book ("Dearly beloved, we are gathered together," "ashes to ashes, dust to dust"), and also some of the most poignant.

It is a section of the Prayer Book that is rarely used by individuals, and that is a pity. For here we find ways to express our great joy in those memorable moments of our lives. Here, too, we find words to get us through those most difficult times when we ourselves have no adequate words to convey our pain. The great message of the pages that follow is that you and I are never, ever alone. Emmanuel, "God with us," truly is with us, laughing with us, weeping with us, carrying us when we feel weak.

❖ Both the state and the status of marriage have been the subject of much discussion in the early years of the twenty-first century. But this is hardly new. The fact is that the BCP in all its iterations through the centuries has offered some of the most profound things to say about matrimony.

1 The 1979 Prayer Book made a change from its predecessors in noting that the primary purpose of marriage is not procreation, but rather the "mutual joy" of the spouses as well as the "help and comfort" they offer one another. The propagation of children is seen as something that is not to be automatically assumed. It should also be noted that while "husband and wife," as well as "man and woman," are used in the 1979 BCP, the question of same-sex marriage has received much attention and debate in recent years in the Episcopal Church, in other parts of the Anglican Communion, in faith communities of all types, and in civil society. A clear resolution regarding this issue is still a work in progress.

2 The 2004 Irish Prayer Book notes that marriage does not occur in a social vacuum. Spouses begin a new life "in the community." They are part of a larger whole. This understanding challenges some modern tendencies toward an often superficial individualism. Many Africans speak of *ubuntu*, which says that "I am because you are." A couple's commitment to one another has a ripple effect far beyond them. For this reason, the community is called to pray for, and actively support, those who are making their wedding vows.

3 What a beautiful image! Spouses as "ministers ... of reconciliation and change." Love is manifested in forgiveness and reassurance, and so each spouse can dare to dig deeper and be challenged.

The union of husband and wife in heart, body, and mind is intended by God for their mutual joy; for the help and comfort given one another in prosperity and adversity; and, when it is God's will, for the procreation of children and their nurture in the knowledge of the Lord.[1] Therefore marriage is not to be entered into unadvisedly or lightly, but reverently, deliberately, and in accordance with the purposes for which it was instituted by God.

FROM THE CELEBRATION AND BLESSING OF A MARRIAGE

In marriage husband and wife begin a new life together in the community.[2] It is a permanent commitment that all should honour. It must not be undertaken carelessly, lightly or selfishly, but by God's help, with reverence, responsibility, respect, and the promise to be faithful.

FROM THE 2004 IRISH BOOK OF COMMON PRAYER

Eternal love never fails; our love needs to forgive and be forgiven. As we pray and forgive we minister reconciliation. Those who marry are God's ministers to each other of reconciliation and change.[3] As they grow together, wife and husband foster one another's strengths, they provide each other with the reassurance and love needed to overcome their weaknesses.

FROM THE 1989 NEW ZEALAND PRAYER BOOK

❖ It is a testament to the power of the Prayer Book's linguistic legacy that its words for Holy Matrimony are so often used in cinematic depictions of weddings. These questions and answers come in the early section of the service, immediately following the preamble that explains the purpose of marriage and the challenge for any possible objector to "speak now; or else for ever hold your peace." These are not the vows themselves, but rather are known as the spouses' declaration of consent, saying up front that they each are ready and prepared to make their vows, which will come later, after the scripture readings and homily. The declaration of consent originally was made some time before the wedding as a way of saying that the couple was indeed choosing to marry and was not simply being coerced into the union.

4 A significant difference from the movies is that the Prayer Book calls on the spouses to answer the questions put forth to them by saying, "I will," not the more familiar, "I do." The latter is in the present tense: "I do" ... right now. It implicitly assumes that there could be days to come when I am ready to say, "I don't."

The Prayer Book's answer, "I will," goes beyond the present moment. It says "Whatever comes, I will ... not just today, but in all the days to come." In this way, the answer presages the vows that are yet to come in the service.

5 The other key difference is that in the Prayer Book service the members of the congregation are not merely passive spectators watching the scene before them, but rather co-participants, responding to a third question not asked in the movies, declaring their support of the couple by promising to do all in their power to uphold them in their marriage. That "we will" can help struggling spouses get through the difficult times when "I will" just is not enough.

The Celebrant says to the woman
N., will you have this man to be your husband; to live
together in the covenant of marriage? Will you love him,
comfort him, honor and keep him, in sickness and in
health; and, forsaking all others, be faithful to him as long
as you both shall live?

The Woman answers
I will.[4]

The Celebrant says to the man
N., will you have this woman to be your wife; to live
together in the covenant of marriage? Will you love her,
comfort her, honor and keep her, in sickness and in health;
and, forsaking all others, be faithful to her as long as you
both shall live?

The Man answers
I will.

The Celebrant then addresses the congregation, saying
Will all of you witnessing these promises do all in your
power to uphold these two persons in their marriage?
People We will.[5]

FROM THE CELEBRATION AND BLESSING OF A MARRIAGE

❖ The marital vows are among the most recognizable words in the English language: "for better for worse, for richer for poorer, in sickness and in health." The imagery is reminiscent of Saint Paul's words about our union with Christ, when in Romans 8:35 he asks, "Who will separate us from the love of Christ? Will hardship, or distress, or persecution, or famine, or nakedness, or peril, or sword?"

Even so, the Prayer Book reminds us that love is about hanging in there with one another, staying connected, not just in the happy times but even more so in the most difficult times. In this way, we show something far more than human affection; we reveal anew the divine love that never, ever lets us go.

6 The chief change the 1979 BCP and other modern revisions have made to the wedding vows is the elimination of the word "obey" in the wife's version of the vows. In older Prayer Books the woman would add to the promises to "love and cherish" the additional promise to obey her husband, as seen in the 1662 version provided here as well. This was a clear indication of the distinction of roles and the power differential between the genders. Today the vows are interchangeable, and "obey" is no longer included.

7 Exchanging rings is an ancient and highly symbolic part of the marriage service. The traditional words that accompanied the act of the groom placing the ring on the bride's finger spoke of him worshipping her with his body and endowing on her all his worldly goods, as seen in the 1662 version. Today, the spouses' mutual act of exchanging rings includes words that echo those older ones, speaking of "all that I am, and all that I have."

In the Name of God, I, *N.*, take you, *N.*, to be my wife/husband, to have and to hold from this day forward, for better for worse, for richer for poorer, in sickness and in health, to love and to cherish,⁶ until we are parted by death. This is my solemn vow.

N., I give you this ring as a symbol of my vow, and with all that I am, and all that I have, I honor you, in the Name of the Father, and of the Son, and of the Holy Spirit.⁷

Those whom God has joined together let no one put asunder.
Amen.

FROM THE CELEBRATION AND BLESSING OF A MARRIAGE

I, *N.*, take thee *N.* to be my wedded husband, to have and to hold from this day forward, for better for worse, for richer for poorer, in sickness and in health, to love, cherish, and to obey, till death do us part, according to God's holy ordinance; and thereto I give thee my troth.

With this Ring, I thee wed, with my body I thee worship, and with all my worldly goods I thee endow: In the Name of the Father, and of the Son, and of the Holy Ghost.

FROM THE 1662 ENGLISH BOOK OF COMMON PRAYER

❖ Before their family and friends send the newly married couple off amidst a hail of thrown rice and congratulatory cries, they first pause, take a quiet moment, and together pray for them. Here we find a series of prayers that are appropriately used not simply at the start of a couple's life together, but throughout their shared journey. For we always need wisdom and devotion in the ordering of our common life, to grow in love and peace, the grace to forgive and be forgiven.

Each of these prayers can be used on a different night of the week so that, interestingly, the prayer about mutual forgiveness comes mid-week—by that point, the two persons probably need to be forgiven for something! In any case, these prayers can be an ongoing gift for the couple, better than anything bought through the bridal registry. For here we have tiny nuggets of grace to get us through each day ... together.

Give them wisdom and devotion in the ordering of their common life, that each may be to the other a strength in need, a counselor in perplexity, a comfort in sorrow, and a companion in joy. Amen.

Grant that their wills may be so knit together in your will, and their spirits in your Spirit, that they may grow in love and peace with you and one another all the days of their life. Amen.

Give them grace, when they hurt each other, to recognize and acknowledge their fault, and to seek each other's forgiveness and yours. Amen.

Make their life together a sign of Christ's love to this sinful and broken world, that unity may overcome estrangement, forgiveness heal guilt, and joy conquer despair. Amen.

Give them such fulfillment of their mutual affection that they may reach out in love and concern for others. Amen.

FROM THE CELEBRATION AND BLESSING OF A MARRIAGE

❖ The bride and the groom make their vows and exchange rings. The people offer their support and pray for the newly married couple. But before all is said and done, before that familiar kiss between groom and bride that culminates the joyful event, the officiating bishop or priest offers a blessing over the couple.

That blessing is a reminder that there is always a third in our relationships, the Divine One who guides and guards, who provides and protects. There is no promise of an easy life together—quite the opposite, as the vows themselves declare—but in all that we go through, "in [our] sleeping and in [our] waking, in [our] joys and in [our] sorrows," the Unseen is present to "lead [us] into all peace."

8 The images in this blessing reflect the tangible symbols used in the service. The "seal upon their hearts" corresponds to the ring that seals the marriage vows and is forever on their fingers. The "mantle about their shoulders" is like the fine clothes worn by the bride and groom. The crown, a reminder of an old Eastern Orthodox tradition, is now symbolized in the veil sometimes worn by the bride. All of these images and symbols are representations of the love between the couple, a love that ultimately emanates from God's own self.

9 The blessing does not have to end with the conclusion of the wedding service. In the *Book of Occasional Services*, a supplement to the BCP, there is a wonderful service for the Celebration for a Home, in which each room in the house is dedicated to God's service and both the home and its inhabitants are blessed. Some couples place a small plaque, picture, or even a Holy Water font at the entrance of their home to recognize that God was not just present at the beginning of their life together, but remains an ongoing "inhabitant" in their home.

By the power of your Holy Spirit, pour out the abundance of your blessing upon this man and this woman. Defend them from every enemy. Lead them into all peace. Let their love for each other be a seal upon their hearts, a mantle about their shoulders, and a crown upon their foreheads.[8] Bless them in their work and in their companionship; in their sleeping and in their waking; in their joys and in their sorrows; in their life and in their death. Finally, in your mercy, bring them to that table where your saints feast for ever in your heavenly home; through Jesus Christ our Lord, who with you and the Holy Spirit lives and reigns, one God, for ever and ever. Amen.

FROM THE CELEBRATION AND BLESSING OF A MARRIAGE

Almighty and everlasting God, grant to this home the grace of your presence, that you may be known to be the inhabitant of this dwelling, and the defender of this household; through Jesus Christ our Lord, who with you and the Holy Spirit lives and reigns, one God, for ever and ever. Amen.[9]

FROM THE CELEBRATION FOR A HOME SERVICE,
IN THE BOOK OF OCCASIONAL SERVICES

❖ Psalm 127:3 says, "Sons are indeed a heritage from the Lord...." The Prayer Book and its supplemental *Book of Occasional Services* reflect this sentiment, offering prayers both during the time of pregnancy and following the child's birth. As with so many of the other prayers herein, these can be helpful tools used by the parents or parents-to-be: "We give you thanks for the blessing you have bestowed upon us in giving us a child ..."

10 There is no suggestion here of political viewpoints on the controversial question of abortion. The Prayer Book and its supplements instead assume pregnancy as a providential gift and, following precedents in both Hebrew and Christian scriptures, place both mother and unborn child in the hands of God. In more recent years, prayers have been developed for those difficult times when miscarriages occur.

11 For the parents, what is needed is "calm strength and patient wisdom." How very true! It is not easy to raise and nurture our children. To find the grace needed when our own inner resources are depleted is not just important, but crucial. The ultimate goal is to help our children love those wonderful qualities outlined herein, a list that recalls Saint Paul's words in Philippians 4:8: "Finally, beloved, whatever is true, whatever is honorable, whatever is just, whatever is pure, whatever is pleasing, whatever is commendable, if there is any excellence and if there is anything worthy of praise, think about these things."

O Lord and giver of life, receive our prayer for N. and for
the child she has conceived, that they may happily come to
the time of birth,**10** and serving you in all things may rejoice
in your loving providence. We ask this through our Lord
Jesus Christ, who lives and reigns with you and the Holy
Spirit, one God, now and for ever. Amen.

FROM THE BLESSING OF A PREGNANT WOMAN,
IN THE BOOK OF OCCASIONAL SERVICES

O God, you have taught us through your blessed Son
that whoever receives a little child in the name of Christ
receives Christ himself: We give you thanks for the blessing
you have bestowed upon this family in giving them a child.
Confirm their joy by a lively sense of your presence with
them, and give them calm strength and patient wisdom
as they seek to bring this child to love all that is true and
noble, just and pure, lovable and gracious, excellent and
admirable,**11** following the example of our Lord and Savior,
Jesus Christ. Amen.

FROM THE THANKSGIVING FOR THE BIRTH OR ADOPTION OF A CHILD

❖ In the 1549 BCP, a rubric, or instruction, like this was offered in the prayers for the sick. Some subsequent revisions placed it in the service at the time of death. But the decision by the compilers of the 1979 Prayer Book to place the rubric here instead, at the end of the service of Thanksgiving for the Birth or Adoption of a Child, feels right and certainly is more forward thinking.

We all have a responsibility to the future, and parents especially need to consider the well-being of their children after they themselves are gone. The call to make provision early on, long before any signs of impending decline and death, is not only practical but also a faith statement about mortality and resurrection. All too often, ministers are nervous about approaching such matters with their congregation, and yet it is a blessed opportunity for all involved to consider their own place in the ongoing cycle of life.

The Minister of the Congregation is directed to instruct the people, from time to time, about the duty of Christian parents to make prudent provision for the well-being of their families, and of all persons to make wills, while they are in health, arranging for the disposal of their temporal goods, not neglecting, if they are able, to leave bequests for religious and charitable uses.

FROM THE THANKSGIVING FOR THE BIRTH OR ADOPTION OF A CHILD

❖ People are often surprised that the Episcopal Church has a rite for private confession. That seems to many to be something associated solely with Roman Catholics. The fact is that most Episcopalians likely do not make use of this opportunity. But make no mistake, this is indeed a wonderful opportunity. The unwritten rule about private confession is "All may, some should, none must." Thus, Reconciliation of a Penitent, as the service is named, is available but not required.

For many individuals who may not even know it, that "some should" applies to them, for while it is always possible to lift up to God pleas for forgiveness, the fact is that for many individuals, things are not real until they are spoken aloud and heard by another flesh-and-blood human being. Counselors, therapists, twelve-step program coordinators will all assert: there is something powerful about unloading one's baggage, admitting one's failings, unburdening one's conscience. And then, there is incredible release in hearing aloud the words of absolution and the challenge to start anew. It calls to mind once more Jesus's words to many people who came to him weighed down with guilt, "Neither do I condemn you. Go your way, and from now on do not sin again" (John 8:11).

12 The Prayer Book rubrics instruct that if confession is made to someone other than a priest or bishop, then in place of this absolution is instead a declaration of forgiveness. This is because of the power of the word "absolve," which means to know that our sins are "put away" as if they had never been.

13 This closing line on the part of the priest who just declared absolution to the penitent is poignant, as it is a reminder that we are fellow sinners ... and fellow beloved, absolved children of God.

Bless me, for I have sinned.

Our Lord Jesus Christ, who has left power to his Church to absolve all sinners who truly repent and believe in him, of his great mercy forgive you all your offences; and by his authority committed to me, I absolve you from all your sins: In the Name of the Father, and of the Son, and of the Holy Spirit. Amen.[12]

The Lord has put away all your sins.

Go in peace, and pray for me, a sinner.[13]

FROM THE RECONCILIATION OF A PENITENT

❖ The Christian scripture letter of James 5:14 says the following: "Are any among you sick? They should call for the elders of the church and have them pray over them, anointing them with oil in the Name of the Lord." Through the centuries, anointing the sick has continued, and taken on a sacramental notion, as oil set aside for this purpose is the outward and visible sign of the power of the Divine Presence for the inward and spiritual grace that is healing, wholeness—what the ancient Hebrews called *shalom*—even if the physical sickness is not cured.

This is the paradox of anointing the sick: it doesn't always work. Sometimes there are visible miracles, which catch our attention and make our jaws drop. But all too often the prayers are not answered, at least not in the physical sense that we can see and examine. The healing can and often does happen on a level that is not visible, but still deeply real and transformative.

14 Here we see a curious thing that we find in the Gospel stories as well, such as when a group of friends bring a lame man to Jesus, who proceeds to look at the man and say, "Your sins are forgiven" (Matthew 9:2). The crowd is shocked, but Jesus seems to have recognized the spiritual healing that the man desperately needed. At the same time, we cannot reduce this to the idea that good people stay well and become prosperous while bad people get sick and face difficulties. This is not helpful, for as we all well know, good people do get sick, lose jobs, and face numerous heartaches.

But our God is always with us. We are never alone.

15 This poignant prayer from the church in Aotearoa/New Zealand speaks to those who are aging, who are facing the uncertainties of "life's last quarter."

N., I anoint you with oil in the Name of the Father, and of the Son, and of the Holy Spirit. Amen.

As you are outwardly anointed with this holy oil, so may our heavenly Father grant you the inward anointing of the Holy Spirit. Of his great mercy, may he forgive you your sins,[14] release you from suffering, and restore you to wholeness and strength. May he deliver you from all evil, preserve you in all goodness, and bring you to everlasting life; through Jesus Christ our Lord. Amen.

FROM THE MINISTRATION TO THE SICK

God of the unknown,
as age draws in on us, irresistible as the tide,
make our life's last quarter the best that there has been.
As our strength ebbs, release our inner vitality,
all you have taught us over the years;
as our energy diminishes
increase our compassion, and educate our prayer.
You have made us human to share your divine life;
grant us the first-fruits;
make our life's last quarter the best that there has been.
Amen.[15]

PRAYER FOR PEOPLE AGING, FROM THE NEW ZEALAND PRAYER BOOK

❖ There is no time, perhaps, when it is more important to offer prayer and the promise of God's presence than when a person leaves this world and enters the larger life. Such times are difficult, perhaps overwhelming. The fact is that despite our weekly profession of faith in the "resurrection of the body and the life everlasting," we usually act as if we believe in immortality instead of death and resurrection, as if we are going to go on and on without ever dying.

There is a fear that underlies all this, but this fear can be swallowed up in Charles Wesley's hymn "Love Divine, all loves excelling." That love stands with us as we move through the valley of the shadow of death, and that same love blows away the stone from the tomb and lets the dawn of resurrection life burst through. It is not enough to say, as Saint Paul declared, "Where, O death, is your sting?" (1 Corinthians 15:55).

16 This prayer of commendation to God, as well as the one immediately below it, was first found in the American Prayer Book of 1928, although both prayers go back to the ancient Sarum rites that preceded even the earliest BCP. Here we see the soul of the deceased commended to the Triune God. It is an extraordinary moment when we witness the breath of life go out of a person, and this is a poignant way of marking that moment.

17 This second commendatory prayer is also included at the end of the burial service in the 1979 BCP. Unlike the prayer above, which opens more as a bold command to the departing soul, this one is clearly a plea on that soul's behalf to a "merciful Savior."

Depart, O Christian soul, out of this world;
In the Name of God the Father Almighty who created you;
In the Name of Jesus Christ who redeemed you;
In the Name of the Holy Spirit who sanctifies you.
May your rest be this day in peace,
and your dwelling place in the Paradise of God.[16]

Into your hands, O merciful Savior, we commend your servant N. Acknowledge, we humbly beseech you, a sheep of your own fold, a lamb of your own flock, a sinner of your own redeeming. Receive him into the arms of your mercy, into the blessed rest of everlasting peace, and into the glorious company of the saints in light. Amen.[17]

May his soul, and the souls of all the departed, through the mercy of God, rest in peace. Amen.

FROM THE MINISTRATION AT THE TIME OF DEATH

❖ Ours is a sure and certain hope, a gift provided by the One who has gone through the darkness before us. Because he lives, as the old hymn says, "I can face tomorrow." Because death itself has met its match in the resurrection of Jesus, we truly need fear nothing anymore. All our fears and anxieties have at their core some notion of our own mortality. Far from glossing over our eventual death, each recital of these words is a glorious creed. God is not done with us yet, even after death. Our hope is a strong hope, a courageous hope.

18 Cranmer's 1549 Prayer Book began the burial service with a procession and this short passage from the Gospel of John 11:25, followed by the burial itself, an office of prayers, and the Eucharist, while his 1552 revision abbreviated the entire service.

This Gospel passage is about the death of Lazarus, Jesus's friend. When Lazarus's sisters ask Jesus where he was when their brother died, Jesus responded with this powerful "I am" statement. These same words can be a source of hope when we face moments of death and wonder where Jesus is.

19 It is significant that these words come from the Book of Job (19:25–27), after the title character has lost everyone and everything he holds dear, after he has listened to the platitudes and even admonitions from his so-called friends. In the midst of his own understandable complaints and lamentation, Job makes this faith statement about the One who is indeed a "friend and not a stranger."

20 This stanza comes from Paul's First Letter to the Corinthians.

21 What more appropriate close to this processional hymn than these words from the final book of the Bible, the Revelation to John 14:13. Death, for the believer, is rest and peace.

I am Resurrection and I am Life, says the Lord.
Whoever has faith in me shall have life,
even though he die.[18]

As for me, I know that my Redeemer lives
and that at the last he will stand upon the earth.
After my awaking, he will raise me up;
and in my body I shall see God.
I myself shall see, and my eyes behold him
who is my friend and not a stranger.[19]

For none of us has life in himself,
and none becomes his own master when he dies.
For if we have life, we are alive in the Lord,
and if we die, we die in the Lord.
So, then, whether we live or die,
we are the Lord's possession.[20]

Happy from now on
are those who die in the Lord!
So it is, says the Spirit,
for they rest from their labors.[21]

FROM THE BURIAL OF THE DEAD RITE II

❖ We are all interconnected. Family members and close friends walk with us in the journey of life, and when they leave us, we are understandably bereft. These prayers from the Burial Office put words to the deep feelings of grief that can threaten to overwhelm us. In faith and in hope, we affirm that our tearful goodbyes now will one day give way to a joyful reunion. These words are meant to carry us through this in-between time.

22 A slightly revised version of a prayer from the 1928 BCP, this collect for use at the burial of a child has as its source a prayer in the Scottish Prayer Book of 1912. That prayer was more direct in making a connection between Jesus taking the children into his arms and God taking this child for whom we mourn "into the arms of thy love." The current prayer stops short of such a statement, which for grieving parents can be too much to hear, as when well-intentioned friends dare to say that "God needed your child more than you do." This collect instead speaks of us entrusting the child to God's "never-failing care and love," a more sensitive pastoral approach.

23 Although this prayer is also new to the 1979 BCP, one phrase in it, "and strength to meet the days to come," can be found in the Church of England's 1662 Prayer Book. That strength comes from the divine love that surrounds us in the midst of our loss.

24 This prayer from the New Zealand Prayer Book is frank in its cry for help. In speaking of our "shock and grief and confusion of heart," it is an honest and heartfelt plea that could have leapt out of the pages of the Psalms.

O God, whose beloved Son took children into his arms and blessed them: Give us grace to entrust N. to your never-failing care and love, and bring us all to your heavenly kingdom; through Jesus Christ our Lord, who lives and reigns with you and the Holy Spirit, one God, now and for ever. Amen.[22]

Most merciful God, whose wisdom is beyond our under-standing: Deal graciously with NN. in their grief. Surround them with your love, that they may not be overwhelmed by their loss, but have confidence in your goodness, and strength to meet the days to come; through Jesus Christ our Lord. Amen.[23]

COLLECTS FROM THE BURIAL OF THE DEAD RITE II

God of hope, we come to you in shock and grief and con-fusion of heart. Help us to find peace in the knowledge of your loving mercy to all your children, and give us light to guide us out of our darkness into the assurance of your love. Amen.[24]

FROM THE FUNERAL LITURGIES OF THE NEW ZEALAND PRAYER BOOK

4 ☐ Called to Serve

The next major section of the 1979 Prayer Book is designated as "Episcopal Services." This is not a reference to the denomination, but rather taps into the origin of the word "episcopal," which literally means "bishop." While this church lifts up the ministry of laypersons, at the same time it recognizes that there are important ways in which bishops have historically served and continue to serve as chief pastors and overseers. The services in this section of the BCP, therefore, are those where only a bishop can serve as the officiant. These include ordinations of other bishops, priests, and deacons; celebrations of new ministries; and the consecrations of church facilities.

Having said this, it is quickly apparent in reading the following passages that they have much to say to all God's people, not just the ordained. True, not all are called to be bishops, priests, or deacons, but all of us are called in our baptism to serve God and God's creation. There may be a word or a phrase that is used in an ordination service that inspires and challenges you in your own life and ministry.

❖ "Are all apostles? Are all prophets? Are all teachers? ..." (1 Corinthians 12:29). Saint Paul was clear both here and in messages to other first-century churches that different members of the Body of Christ are endowed with different gifts and therefore should fill different roles for the sake of the whole Body. Today, Episcopalians and Anglicans throughout the world recognize and affirm four orders of ministry: laity, bishops, priests, and deacons. All four share the Baptismal Covenant as the ground of all Christian ministry, but the latter three orders are marked by a further process in which they are ordained and consecrated by a bishop for the particular type of ministry to which they are called.

1 From earliest times, ordination has involved the laying on of hands by the bishop (or three bishops, in the case of the ordination of a new bishop). Other actions have at times been added, including the anointing with oil and the dressing with vestments suitable to that office, but it is the laying on of hands that remains the crucial and continuous piece.

It should also be noted that ordinations do not happen in a vacuum, but rather there is a period of discernment, preparation, and training that goes into each process resulting in ordination. The specific requirements are outlined in the church's canons, or governing rules, with additional conditions marked by the local diocese.

2 Anglicans have long affirmed that we are but one part of the larger Body of Christ, and as such recognize the orders of many other Christian denominations. Indeed, the word "catholic," spelled in lowercase, actually means "universal." Although we try not to "re-ordain" unless necessary, we often require some form of Anglican formation and education in order to acclimate those incoming ministers to our heritage and ways of being.

The Holy Scriptures and ancient Christian writers make it clear that from the apostles' time, there have been different ministries within the Church. In particular, since the time of the New Testament, three distinct orders of ordained ministers have been characteristic of Christ's holy catholic Church.

The persons who are chosen and recognized by the Church as being called by God to the ordained ministry are admitted to these sacred orders by solemn prayer and the laying on of episcopal hands.[1]

It is also recognized and affirmed that the threefold ministry is not the exclusive property of this portion of Christ's catholic Church, but is a gift from God for the nurture of his people and the proclamation of his Gospel everywhere.[2]

FROM THE PREFACE TO THE ORDINATION RITES

We stand within a tradition in which there are deacons, priests, and bishops. They are called and empowered to fulfill an ordained ministry and to enable the whole mission of the Church. Our authority is in Scripture and in the Church's continuing practice through the ages.

FROM THE NEW ZEALAND PRAYER BOOK

3 There is much singing, praying, and speaking by many people at an ordination service, but this is the quiet moment when the person to be ordained stands before God and all those present and makes a solemn lifetime vow. It is about spiritual grounding of our vocation and the allegiance of a lifetime. The main section of the Declaration—"I solemnly declare ..."—remains the same in the ordination services for priests and deacons, though they do not include the preamble found in the service for bishops.

4 Many people have admitted that this is their single favorite prayer in the entire BCP, one that is used at every ordination service and sometimes on other occasions as well. It speaks beautifully of the power of the Divine to turn things upside down, or rather right side up, and therefore gives hope to those who are feeling downcast, old, and thoroughly imperfect. Despite its faults, which at times can seem to be many, the church remains a wonderful instrument of God's saving help for the world.

In the Name of the Father, and of the Son, and of the Holy
Spirit, I, *N.N.*, chosen Bishop of the Church in *N.*, solemnly
declare that I do believe the Holy Scriptures of the Old and
New Testaments to be the Word of God, and to contain
all things necessary to salvation; and I do solemnly engage
to conform to the doctrine, discipline, and worship of The
Episcopal Church.[3]

DECLARATION OF CONFORMITY

O God of unchangeable power and eternal light: Look
favorably on your whole Church, that wonderful and sacred
mystery; by the effectual working of your providence, carry
out in tranquility the plan of salvation; let the whole world
see and know that things which were cast down are being
raised up, and things which had grown old are being made
new, and that all things are being brought to their perfec-
tion by him through whom all things were made, your Son
Jesus Christ our Lord; who lives and reigns with you, in the
unity of the Holy Spirit, one God, for ever and ever. Amen.[4]

COLLECT FOR ORDINATIONS

❖ Successor to the apostles, symbol of unity, chief pastor and teacher, the "ordinary" or "ordaining one"—an episkopos (literally, "overseer") is all these things and more. It has been called a lonely vocation, because though there are many priests, deacons, and laypeople in a diocese, they is only one diocesan bishop, and perhaps if the diocese is large, an assistant bishop or two. Outside of the semi-annual gatherings of the House of Bishops, most of the time, locally, a bishop is without peers. Theirs is the ultimate authority in a diocese, but with it ultimate responsibility as well. As a plaque in one bishop's office says: "The buck stops here."

5 In the ordination services, the word "brother" is italicized, as a reminder that in the Episcopal Church, women are also ordained to all three orders: priest since the 1970s and bishop since the 1980s. Other parts of the Anglican Communion, though not all, also ordain women. Some, most notably the Church of England, ordain as deacon and priest, but not as bishop.

6 A bishop is elected from within a diocese for that diocese—the Bishop of _____—and yet is at the same time a bishop of the "one, holy, catholic, and apostolic Church." Focused on the local, the bishop also belongs to the global and takes part in conventions and synods that have effects far beyond that person's diocesan boundaries.

7 It is interesting to note that while persons to be ordained as priests or deacons are asked if they feel called to that office, bishops-elect are instead asked if they are persuaded. There is an ancient tradition of some persons being chased down and "persuaded" physically by a crowd to become a bishop. Today, the process is a little more civilized, but it is still a distinction worth noting.

My *brother*,[5] the people have chosen you and have affirmed their trust in you by acclaiming your election. A bishop in God's holy Church is called to be one with the apostles in proclaiming Christ's resurrection and interpreting the Gospel, and to testify to Christ's sovereignty as Lord of lords and King of kings.

You are called to guard the faith, unity, and discipline of the Church; to celebrate and to provide for the administration of the sacraments of the New Covenant; to ordain priests and deacons and to join in ordaining bishops; and to be in all things a faithful pastor and wholesome example for the entire flock of Christ.

With your fellow bishops you will share in the leadership of the Church throughout the world.[6] Your heritage is the faith of patriarchs, prophets, apostles, and martyrs, and those of every generation who have looked to God in hope. Your joy will be to follow him who came, not to be served, but to serve, and to give his life a ransom for many.

Are you persuaded that God has called you to the office of bishop?

I am so persuaded.[7]

FROM THE ORDINATION OF A BISHOP

8   After examination, prayer, and silence, the time finally comes. The bishop-elect kneels in front of the presiding bishop, as the other bishops present gather round in a circle. With these words, they lay their hands upon that person, saying together: "Make him/her a bishop in your Church."

Simple, straightforward words ... powerful, profound words. As the rest of the congregation looks on, the tribe surrounding their elders, these successors to the apostles add another to their number.

9   With these words, the other bishops remove their hands and step back, the new bishop remains kneeling, and the presiding bishop prays these words, once more delineating the duties of a bishop and asking that this new shepherd of the flock of Christ present the ultimate offering: "a pure, gentle, and holy life." It is an offering that we all can make, bishops or not.

The final "Amen" is a loud one, as the entire congregation—laity, deacons, priests, bishops, guests, and observers—boldly, gladly, joyfully say "Yes" to what has been done. Immediately hereafter, the new bishop is vested as a priest, but with four crucial additions: a bishop's ring, a pectoral cross, a mitre (the large hat shaped as a tongue of fire like that which appeared over the heads of each of the apostles on Pentecost, as seen in Acts 2), and a crozier, or shepherd's staff.

The apostles have been gone for many centuries, but their successors live on, and with them the heritage of the faith and the Good News of the Reign of God in Jesus Christ.

Therefore, Father, make *N.* a bishop in your Church. Pour out upon *him* the power of your princely Spirit, whom you bestowed upon your beloved Son Jesus Christ, with whom he endowed the apostles, and by whom your Church is built up in every place, to the glory and unceasing praise of your Name.[8]

To you, O Father, all hearts are open; fill, we pray, the heart of this your servant whom you have chosen to be a bishop in your Church, with such love of you and of all the people, that *he* may feed and tend the flock of Christ, and exercise without reproach the high priesthood to which you have called *him*, serving before you day and night in the ministry of reconciliation, declaring pardon in your Name, offering the holy gifts, and wisely overseeing the life and work of the Church. In all things may *he* present before you the acceptable offering of a pure, and gentle, and holy life; through Jesus Christ your Son, to whom, with you and the Holy Spirit, be honor and power and glory in the Church, now and for ever. Amen.[9]

FROM THE ORDINATION OF A BISHOP

❖ The Christian scriptures speak of "bishops and deacons," and the term "presbyter" is found early on in the life of the church. Eventually, the word "priest" was substituted for it, meaning one who presides at the Altar. The priest/presbyter does far more than that. While a bishop oversees a diocese, a collection of many congregations within a geographical boundary, the priest pastors and leads the local flock that is one part of that larger whole.

It is the priest's, not the bishop's, sermons the congregation hears week after week. It is the priest who officiates in moments of celebration at baptisms and weddings, as well as in moments of sorrow at funerals and burials. The priest is the one who is there day in and day out, a fellow pilgrim and a leader along the way.

10 The actual BCP text reads "my brother," but I have changed it here simply to show that, as previously mentioned, all three orders of ordained ministry are available to women as well as men in the Episcopal Church. On July 29, 1974, eleven women were irregularly ordained in Philadelphia, becoming known as the Philadelphia 11. Their ordinations were considered irregular because it was not yet permitted, but in 1976, the General Convention of the Episcopal Church voted to permit women to serve not only as deacons, but as priests and bishops as well. It took another decade before one was elected to serve as bishop.

11 A person who feels called to the priesthood goes through an often lengthy process of discernment on both the congregational and diocesan level, followed by a period of training, either at a seminary or through some alternative formation program.

By the time the person is asked this question in the ordination service—"Do you believe that you are truly called"—the fact is that she or he has likely already answered it a hundred times before along the way.

My [sister],[10] the Church is the family of God, the body of Christ, and the temple of the Holy Spirit. All baptized people are called to make Christ known as Savior and Lord, and to share in the renewing of his world. Now you are called to work as a pastor, priest, and teacher, together with your bishop and fellow presbyters, and to take your share in the councils of the Church.

As a priest, it will be your task to proclaim by word and deed the Gospel of Jesus Christ, and to fashion your life in accordance with its precepts. You are to love and serve the people among whom you work, caring alike for young and old, strong and weak, rich and poor. You are to preach, to declare God's forgiveness to penitent sinners, to pronounce God's blessing, to share in the administration of Holy Baptism and in the celebration of the mysteries of Christ's Body and Blood, and to perform the other ministrations entrusted to you.

In all that you do, you are to nourish Christ's people from the riches of his grace, and strengthen them to glorify God in this life and in the life to come.

My [sister], do you believe that you are truly called by God and his Church to this priesthood?

I believe I am so called.[11]

FROM THE ORDINATION OF A PRIEST

12 As the priest-to-be kneels, the bishop lays hands on that person's head, and all other priests/presbyters present join in the laying on of hands, a symbol of sharing in that priestly office. Together, then, they join the bishop in saying these words.

13 As the other priests remove their hands and step back, the ordaining bishop continues with this prayer for the new priest, once more naming the roles this person has been ordained to fulfill: "faithful pastor, patient teacher, wise councilor." To serve God and the people "without reproach," this is the goal.

14 The people affirm the bishop's prayer for the priest with a bold "Amen!" Following this, the new priest is vested with a stole, something like a scarf, placed around her or his neck, the long ends falling straight down in front. It has been likened to the yoke that is placed on the shoulders of oxen as they carry the load assigned to them. Even so, with the placing of Christ's yoke on the shoulders of the priest, it is easy to call to mind the Savior's words in Matthew's Gospel: "Take my yoke upon you, and learn from me" (11:29).

Therefore, Father, through Jesus Christ your Son, give your Holy Spirit to N.; fill [*her*] with grace and power, and make *her* a priest in your Church.[12]

May [*she*] exalt you, O Lord, in the midst of your people; offer spiritual sacrifices acceptable to you; boldly proclaim the gospel of salvation; and rightly administer the sacraments of the New Covenant. Make [*her*] a faithful pastor, a patient teacher, and a wise councilor. Grant that in all things [*she*] may serve without reproach,[13] so that your people may be strengthened and your Name glorified in all the world. All this we ask through Jesus Christ our Lord, who with you and the Holy Spirit lives and reigns, one God, for ever and ever. Amen.[14]

FROM THE ORDINATION OF A PRIEST

❖ The office of deacon is one that seemingly disappeared for many years, even centuries, only to be rediscovered by the church in recent times. Although a practice developed long ago that persons to be ordained priests must first serve for a given time in this office, leading to the term "transitional deacons," the fact is that the diaconate is a very different, and special, ordained ministry. Its origins, it is said, may be found in Acts 6, when the apostles laid hands on seven persons selected from among the Greek-speaking believers in Jerusalem, to make sure that their pastoral needs would not be neglected. Immediately, one of those seven, Stephen, preached a strong, hard-hitting sermon that got him killed by those who did not want to hear what he had to say.

In many ways, deacons are called to continue that ministry of challenge as well as compassion, to ensure that the needy are noticed and cared for, not just by them but by all the church.

15 As mentioned already, women as well as men may be ordained in the Episcopal Church as deacon, priest, or bishop.

16 A deacon may be assigned to a parish, but she or he ultimately remains under the authority of the bishop. What is different is the preparation and training of persons for the diaconate, as this usually takes place through diocesan-sponsored formation programs, not seminaries.

17 It is important to note that the Prayer Book stipulates that deacons are to "assist the bishop and priests in public worship," not lead it themselves. A deacon is expected to read the Gospel, call on the people to confess their sins, set the Altar, and proclaim the dismissal but is not allowed to preside at the Eucharist or offer a blessing or absolution. It is an assisting ministry, a servant ministry, a crucial ministry that bridges the church with the world.

My *brother*,[15] every Christian is called to follow Jesus Christ, serving God the Father, through the power of the Holy Spirit. God now calls you to a special ministry of servanthood directly under your bishop.[16] In the name of Jesus Christ, you are to serve all people, particularly the poor, the weak, the sick, and the lonely.

As a deacon in the Church, you are to study the Holy Scriptures, to seek nourishment from them, and to model your life upon them. You are to make Christ and his redemptive love known, by your word and example, to those among whom you live, and work, and worship. You are to interpret to the Church the needs, concerns, and hopes of the world. You are to assist the bishop and priests in public worship and in the ministration of God's Word and Sacraments,[17] and you are to carry out other duties assigned to you from time to time. At all times, your life and teaching are to show Christ's people that in serving the helpless they are serving Christ himself.

My *brother*, do you believe that you are truly called by God and his Church to the life and work of a deacon?

I believe I am so called.

From The Ordination of a Deacon

18 The person to be ordained kneels in front of the bishop, who alone lays hands on the person's head and says these ordaining words. This is to signify that this special servant of God reports directly to the bishop, not to a congregation or priest.

19 As with Stephen and Philip the Deacon, another member of the seven Greek-speakers set apart by the apostles for the ministry of service in Acts 6, humility combines with strength in the life and ministry of any deacon. This person will always be called to have a foot in the church and a foot in the hurting world around it. Philip goes on in Acts to share the Gospel with a foreigner who might not even have been approached by some other believers. The allusion to the Son of Man as One who came "not to be served, but to serve" goes back to Mark's Gospel 10:45.

20 Following the bold "Amen!" of the people at the end of the prayers, the new deacon is then vested, particularly with a stole that is worn over one shoulder, crossing the chest, with the two ends secured together. This is different from priests and bishops, who have both ends hanging down in front. The image of the deacon is of one ready to work, ready to serve.

Therefore, Father, through Jesus Christ your Son, give your Holy Spirit to N.; fill *him* with grace and power, and make *him* a deacon in your Church.[18]

Make *him*, O Lord, modest and humble, strong and constant, to observe the discipline of Christ. Let *his* life and teaching so reflect your commandments, that through *him* many may come to know you and love you. As your Son came not to be served but to serve,[19] may this deacon share in Christ's service, and come to the unending glory of him who, with you and the Holy Spirit, lives and reigns, one God, for ever and ever. Amen.[20]

FROM THE ORDINATION OF A DEACON

❖ Although this prayer is usually reserved for when a priest formally begins a new ministry at a parish, there are parts of it that can easily and appropriately speak for us as we begin each day: "O Lord my God, I am not worthy to have you come under my roof; yet to you and your service I devote myself, body, soul, and spirit. Make me an instrument of your salvation for all those entrusted to my care. May all the desires of my heart and will center in what you would have me do today."

In essence, every day is a celebration of a new ministry; every day offers new opportunities to experience and share God's grace, whoever we are and wherever we find ourselves. It is like the marquee of a parish church I once passed that read: "Rector: the Rev. David Johnson / Ministers: All the people." You and I are ministers ... all the time. To God and to God's service I indeed devote myself, body, soul, and spirit.

O Lord my God, I am not worthy to have you come under my roof; yet you have called your servant to stand in your house, and to serve at your altar. To you and to your service I devote myself, body, soul, and spirit. Fill my memory with the record of your mighty works; enlighten my understanding with the light of your Holy Spirit; and may all the desires of my heart and will center in what you would have me do. Make me an instrument of your salvation for the people entrusted to my care, and grant that I may faithfully administer your holy Sacraments, and by my life and teaching set forth your true and living Word. Be always with me in carrying out the duties of my ministry. In prayer, quicken my devotion; in praises, heighten my love and gratitude; in preaching, give me readiness of thought and expression; and grant that, by the clearness and brightness of your holy Word, all the world may be drawn into your blessed kingdom. All this I ask for the sake of your Son our Savior Jesus Christ. Amen.

FROM THE CELEBRATION OF A NEW MINISTRY

❖ What a beautiful hymn for any time and any place, especially when facing a new task, a new challenge. It is a plea for the Spirit to come and fill us anew, anointing and "cheering" our weary body, our "soiled face." We do not need to attend an ordination to chant this hymn. It can be our own, as it was used in past centuries as a private prayer.

21 The Latin hymn dates back to the ninth century, attributed to Rabanus Maurus, abbot at Fulda and archbishop of Mainz. In medieval times it was used primarily in the Daily Office on Pentecost as well as a personal prayer of preparation by priests before presiding at Mass. It has been a part of Anglican ordination services since Cranmer first included an English translation in his 1550 Ordinal. It was included, though with a different translation, in the 1662 BCP as part of the Ordering of Priests and Consecration of Bishops.

It is a metered chant and either sung as versicle and response or done in unison.

22 Although in earlier versions of the Prayer Book the hymn occupied a different place in the ordination services for priests and bishops, in the 1979 BCP it is specified after the examination of the ordinand. The person kneels, and as the hymn is chanted the ordaining ones gather around in preparation for the laying on of hands.

The Prayer Book allows as an alternative another hymn, *Veni Sancte Spiritus*, often attributed to Archbishop of Canterbury Stephen Langton around 1200. Whichever hymn is used, it is followed by a period of silence before the prayer of consecration begins.

Come, Holy Ghost, our souls inspire,
  and lighten with celestial fire.
Thou the anointing Spirit art,
  who dost thy seven-fold gifts impart.
Thy blessed Unction from above
  is comfort, life, and fire of love.
Enable with perpetual light
  the dullness of our blinded sight.
Anoint and cheer our soiled face
  with the abundance of thy grace.
Keep far our foes, give peace at home:
  where thou art guide, no ill can come.
Teach us to know the Father, Son,
  and thee, of both, to be but One;
That through the ages all along,
  this may be our endless song:
Praise to thy eternal merit,
  Father, Son, and Holy Spirit.[21]

VENI CREATOR SPIRITUS, FROM THE ORDINATION SERVICES[22]

❖ The Consecration of a Church and the Celebration for a Home share in common the conviction that God blesses and sanctifies places. Although we concur with Stephen, the first martyr, in Acts 7 that God is everywhere and does not need a temple made by human hands in which to dwell, we also recognize the reality of sacred space. The beauty is that it does not have to be a church or synagogue. Even as the bishop offers a blessing on a church as a place set apart (which is what "sanctify" literally means), so we can ask for a priest surrounded by friends and family to help us mark our home as a place set apart for welcome and peace.

23 The practice of the bishop praying over a church finds its antecedent in King David kneeling at the site of the future temple in Jerusalem and asking God's blessing, seen in 1 Chronicles 29.

24 The bishop makes with his crozier, or shepherd's staff, the sign of the cross at the doorway while saying these words.

25 Unlike the dedication of a church, for the blessing of a home a priest can and usually is the officiant. A Eucharist can be part of the service, held there in the living room or dining room after the various rooms have all been blessed.

26 Early in the service, this prayer of exorcism can be used, especially in a place where there has been some history of hurt or harm. The goal always is for the home to be a place in which God is clearly present and love prevails.

Almighty God, we thank you for making us in your image, to share in the ordering of your world. Receive the work of our hands in this place, now to be set apart for your worship, the building up of the living, and the remembrance of the dead, to the praise and glory of your Name; through Jesus Christ our Lord. Amen.[23]

Let the door(s) be opened.

Peace be to this house, and to all who enter here: In the Name of the Father, and of the Son, and of the Holy Spirit. Amen.[24]

FROM THE DEDICATION AND CONSECRATION OF A CHURCH

Almighty and everlasting God, grant to this home the grace of your presence, that you may be known to be the inhabitant of this dwelling, and the defender of this household; through Jesus Christ our Lord, who with you and the Holy Spirit lives and reigns, one God, for ever and ever. Amen.[25]

Let the mighty power of the Holy God be present in this place to banish from it every unclean spirit, to cleanse it from every residue of evil, and to make it a secure habitation for those who dwell in it; in the Name of Jesus Christ our Lord. Amen.[26]

CELEBRATION FOR A HOME, FROM THE BOOK OF OCCASIONAL SERVICES

❖ This beautiful litany is almost hidden, stuck as it were at the back section of the Prayer Book, and rarely used, since most people will only experience one consecration of a church, if they experience one at all. It is a shame, as it is a beautiful witness of how much the sacred space of a faith community can mean to its members.

Indeed, the litany is more about community than it is about buildings, speaking of our spiritual adoption and ongoing refreshment, the fulfilling of our desires, the pardon of our sins, the blessing of our vows, and the crowning of our years ... all under the watchful eyes of a loving, always present God.

27 This final stanza comes directly from David's prayer of thanksgiving in 1 Chronicles 29:11, after he had arranged for the building of the future temple. After several prayers that express thanks to God for being with us in so many ways and at so many times, this final doxology, this song of praise that concludes the litany, brings us back to the reality that God is indeed the great, glorious, and majestic One whom we adore.

For making us your children by adoption and grace, and refreshing us day by day with the bread of life.
We thank you, Lord.

For the knowledge of your will and the grace to perform it,
We thank you, Lord.

For the fulfilling of our desires and petitions as you see best for us,
We thank you, Lord.

For the pardon of our sins, which restores us to the company of your faithful people,
We thank you, Lord.

For the blessing of our vows and the crowning of our years with your goodness,
We thank you, Lord.

For the faith of those who have gone before us and for our encouragement by their perseverance,
We thank you, Lord.

Yours, O Lord, is the greatness, the power, the glory, the victory, and the majesty;
For everything in heaven and on earth is yours.
Yours, O Lord, is the kingdom;
And you are exalted as head over all. Amen.[27]

A LITANY OF THANKSGIVING FOR A CHURCH

5 □ Praise and Petition

The final pages of The Book of Common Prayer are full of wonderful resources for individuals as well as groups to use in their devotional life. These pages begin with the Psalter. It has been noted that the Prayer Book is full of Holy Scripture, but here we have an entire book of the Bible included.

This is followed by a collection of prayers and thanksgivings for a variety of occasions. There are prayers for the church and prayers for the nation, prayers for special events and prayers for everyday life. A few are included here, but truly this is a section of the Prayer Book that can be explored in great depth.

Next comes the Catechism of the Church, a question-and-answer teaching tool that puts forth Christian doctrine in an approachable manner. Several key historical documents of the church follow this, including the preface to the 1549 BCP. These documents connect us with our rich and complex heritage.

Finally there are the lectionaries for both Sunday services and the Daily Office. In more recent editions of the 1979 BCP, the Sunday readings are from the Revised Common Lectionary (RCL), which was adopted by the General Convention of the Episcopal Church in 2006 in collaboration with many other Christian denominations who use the RCL.

From start to finish, therefore, the Prayer Book is full of treasures to be discovered and used. These final pages might prove to be among the most valuable for many individuals who herein find just the right psalm or prayer to take with them on the journey.

❖ The Psalter is the original hymnbook, a collection of 150 songs of praise and poignant pleas, some composed three thousand years ago by a young shepherd-king. If other books in the Bible make us think, the Psalms help us feel or, rather, they give us words to express our feelings. It is hardly a coincidence that as Jesus faced his darkest hour on the cross, he cried out with the opening words from Psalm 22: "My God, my God, why have you forsaken me?"

1 The Psalms have long been used by Christian churches as a kind of interactive engagement with the readings from scripture, appropriately placed in the service of Holy Eucharist immediately after the assigned passage from the Hebrew scriptures. In Morning and Evening Prayer, the Psalm actually comes before all the readings, as canticles are used as sung or said responses after each reading.

2 As noted, the psalms may be sung or said in any one of a number of ways, and the *Hymnal 1982*, a complement to the 1979 BCP, offers different settings for chanting or singing them.

3 The brief selections here are from some of the most well-known and well-beloved psalms including, of course, the 23rd Psalm. This one, attributed to King David, has been used by countless people in distress and especially at times of death. It speaks of the Divine Presence even in the midst of the darkest times. Who does not find comfort in those familiar words, "Though I walk through the valley of the shadow of death, I shall fear no evil; for you are with me" (23:4)?

For those who prefer the traditional version from the King James Bible, that is included not in the Psalter section of the Prayer Book, but earlier in the Burial I service.

The Psalter is a body of liturgical poetry. It is designed for vocal, congregational use, whether by singing or reading.[1] There are several traditional methods of psalmody ... direct recitation, antiphonal recitation, responsorial recitation, responsive recitation.[2]

The Lord is my shepherd;
    I shall not be in want.
He makes me lie down in green pastures
    and leads me beside still waters. (Ps. 23)[3]

God is our refuge and strength,
    a very present help in trouble. (Ps. 46)

O God, you are my God; eagerly I seek you;
    my soul thirsts for you, my flesh faints for you,
    as in a barren and dry land where there is no water. (Ps. 63)

I lift up my eyes to the hills;
    from where is my help to come?
My help comes from the Lord,
    the maker of heaven and earth. (Ps. 121)

FROM THE PSALTER

❖ Nestled between the large section that is the Psalter and the final pages of the Prayer Book that include the Catechism, historical documents, and the lectionaries is a treasure chest within a treasure chest. Entitled "Prayers and Thanksgivings," this small section contains spiritual gems for use in different situations. There are prayers for the world and for the church, prayers for the natural order and for the social order, prayers for the nation and for family.

Christians from other non-Anglican traditions sometimes express their confusion or even concern about our reliance on prepared prayers. "Why don't you just talk to God?" they ask. But anyone who has ever bought a greeting card that had just the right words to express their deepest feelings and reflections knows that sometimes the words prepared by others can reach into our soul and become the words we need to share what is deep within us. Even a cursory glance at this collection of prayers and thanksgivings reveals how, much like the collects earlier in the Prayer Book provide a focus to the scripture readings for given days, so these treasures here at the end of the BCP can help us focus on special occasions and particular situations.

4 While the heavenly harmony may feel elusive and world peace may appear a naïve hope, this prayer strikes a chord with its descriptions of the "arrogance and hatred which infect our hearts" and the "walls that separate us." In making this our daily prayer, perhaps we can at least find our own hearts healed of infection and our own walls broken down.

5 "It takes two to tango," says the old truism. This prayer recognizes this reality and therefore asks God to lead and deliver both "them and us." Only in this way can bridges of peace be built.

O God, you made us in your own image and redeemed
us through Jesus your Son: Look with compassion on the
whole human family; take away the arrogance and hatred
which infect our hearts; break down the walls that separate
us; unite us in bonds of love; and work through our struggle
and confusion to accomplish your purposes on earth; that,
in your good time, all nations and races may serve you
in harmony around your heavenly throne; through Jesus
Christ our Lord. Amen.[4]

PRAYER FOR THE WORLD: #3—
FOR THE HUMAN FAMILY, FROM PRAYERS AND THANKSGIVINGS

O God, the Father of all, whose Son commanded us to love
our enemies: Lead them and us from prejudice to truth;
deliver them and us from hatred, cruelty, and revenge; and
in your good time enable us to stand reconciled before you;
through Jesus Christ our Lord. Amen.[5]

PRAYERS FOR THE WORLD: #6—
FOR OUR ENEMIES, FROM PRAYERS AND THANKSGIVINGS

6 This prayer for Christian unity comes, somewhat ironically, from William Laud, archbishop of Canterbury from 1633–45. I say "ironically," because Laud was a hugely divisive figure who fought tirelessly against the Puritans and inflamed so many against him that it was little surprise when he was eventually beheaded, along with King Charles I, who had relied so heavily on his high-church archbishop. Irony aside, it is perhaps a wonderful reality that such marvelous words come from a person who had his own sets of prejudices and a short temper, in other words, a person like some of us. The prayer is timeless and still speaks to a church that is all too often divided, on the local level and the global level. Perhaps by making this prayer our own we can also find our own hearts softened and become builders of bridges instead of walls.

7 In Romans 13:1, Saint Paul famously, and controversially, called on believers to submit to civil authorities: "Let every person be subject to the governing authorities; for there is no authority except from God, and those authorities that exist have been instituted by God." While Christians ever since have struggled to understand this challenge, especially when living under the rule of tyrants, the tradition of The Book of Common Prayer has always been to call on all Christians, not only in the established Church of England, but in the Episcopal Church and other churches in the Anglican Communion, to pray for those in authority over them.

Praying for leaders in our local, state, and national governments does not mean that we necessarily trust them, support their policies, or personally respect them. It instead means that we know that God is bigger than them and us and can work out the divine purpose through any means, including using civil authorities who may not even recognize that providential hand at work behind the scenes.

Gracious Father, we pray for thy holy Catholic Church. Fill it with all truth, in all truth with all peace. Where it is corrupt, purify it; where it is in error, direct it; where in any thing it is amiss, reform it. Where it is right, strengthen it; where it is in want, provide for it; where it is divided, reunite it; for the sake of Jesus Christ thy Son our Savior. Amen.[6]

PRAYER FOR THE CHURCH: #7—
FOR THE CHURCH, FROM PRAYERS AND THANKSGIVINGS

Almighty God our heavenly Father, send down upon those who hold office in this State (Commonwealth, City, County, Town, _____) the spirit of wisdom, charity, and justice; that with steadfast purpose they may faithfully serve in their offices to promote the well-being of all people; through Jesus Christ our Lord. Amen.[7]

PRAYERS FOR NATIONAL LIFE: #23—
FOR LOCAL GOVERNMENT, FROM PRAYERS AND THANKSGIVINGS

8 This prayer hits hard. In it, we not only pray for "all poor and neglected persons," but we likewise admit that all too often they are easy for us to ignore and neglect. In this way, the prayer is both a compassionate plea for others and a challenge to self. It is not a call for God to remember "all those who have none to care for them"—God already remembers ... and cares. It is instead an intentional choice on our part to join God in remembering them and, even more, to be given the divine help we need to enable us to "turn their sorrow into joy."

What a wonderful example of prayer that breeds action!

9 In several places throughout the 1979 Prayer Book, there are references to our connection with the rest of creation and the need for better stewardship of "this fragile earth, our island home" (as mentioned in Eucharistic Prayer C).

In this prayer for the conservation of natural resources, we claim an even more audacious role not only as stewards, but as God's "fellow workers." Rather than instill arrogance, however, this assumes action on our part, and a plea for the "wisdom and reverence" that need to underlie such action.

Much has been said in recent years of the circle of life and our part in it. But the fact is that the Christian faith has a rich tradition of affirming our interconnectedness with the rest of creation, a tradition best represented perhaps in the legacy of Saint Francis of Assisi. His lyrical celebration of "Brother Sun and Sister Moon" is not only one of the earliest examples of Italian, not Latin, poetry, but also a foundation for much of the environmental work undertaken by Episcopalians and Anglicans today.

Almighty and most merciful God, we remember before you all poor and neglected persons whom it would be easy for us to forget: the homeless and the destitute, the old and the sick, all who have none to care for them. Help us to heal those who are broken in body or spirit, and to turn their sorrow into joy. Grant this, Father, for the love of your Son, who for our sake became poor, Jesus Christ our Lord. Amen.[8]

PRAYERS FOR THE SOCIAL ORDER: #35—
FOR THE POOR AND NEGLECTED, FROM PRAYERS AND THANKSGIVINGS

Almighty God, in giving us dominion over things on earth, you made us fellow workers in your creation: Give us wisdom and reverence so to use the resources of nature, that no one may suffer from our abuse of them, and that generations yet to come may continue to praise you for your bounty; through Jesus Christ our Lord. Amen.[9]

PRAYERS FOR THE NATURAL ORDER: #41—
FOR THE CONSERVATION OF NATURAL RESOURCES,
FROM PRAYERS AND THANKSGIVINGS

10 What parent or teacher could not echo the concern behind these words about the "unsteady and confusing world" in which our young people find themselves? This prayer asks God to do what we all too often are unable to do: to help them see where true life lies!

While some other prayers ask for God to give us the grace to do what we need to do, this prayer seems to presume our helplessness when it comes to those youth in our charge. We can talk and talk, and yet they just don't—or perhaps can't—hear us. So this is a petition for God to whisper to their hearts the things that really matter, the words that will bring life to them.

Of course there is always something we can say or do, but perhaps it is even more important that we speak to God about our children than constantly speak to our children about God and what is good.

11 This little prayer for a birthday can be a delightful gift to share with someone. It is often used by priests during a Sunday service right before or after the Peace, when they invite any people in the congregation having birthdays (and sometimes wedding anniversaries as well) that week to come forward and receive a blessing. But it is one that can be used by anyone anytime, either in person or written down in a card. Imagine how surprised and touched a person feels when they not only receive a birthday card, but a handwritten prayer for them inside. It is also a reminder to them that not only do you care for them, but you believe that God cares for them as well.

God our Father, you see your children growing up in an unsteady and confusing world: Show them that your ways give more life than the ways of the world, and that following you is better than chasing after selfish goals. Help them to take failure, not as a measure of their worth, but as a chance for a new start. Give them strength to hold their faith in you, and to keep alive their joy in your creation; through Jesus Christ our Lord. Amen.[10]

PRAYERS FOR FAMILY AND PERSONAL LIFE: #47—
FOR YOUNG PERSONS, FROM PRAYERS AND THANKSGIVINGS

O God, our times are in your hand: Look with favor, we pray, on your servant N. as he begins another year. Grant that he may grow in wisdom and grace, and strengthen his trust in your goodness all the days of his life; through Jesus Christ our Lord. Amen.[11]

PRAYERS FOR FAMILY AND PERSONAL LIFE: #50—
FOR A BIRTHDAY, FROM PRAYERS AND THANKSGIVINGS

12 Although many of the prayers and thanksgivings in this section of the 1979 BCP are in contemporary English, there are certain prayers that, like the Lord's Prayer or the 23rd Psalm, just resonate with people in the traditional language of "thee's" and "thou's."

So it is with this prayer for guidance, and it is not simply the pronouns that make this a prayer that is easily remembered and much loved, but also the beautiful rhythm therein, as it speaks of our works "begun, continued, and ended in thee." It is for many a mantra that at the same time echoes also the Christian scripture's promise that the One who "began a good work among you will bring it to completion" (Philippians 1:6).

13 Here we find another prayer in traditional language that speaks so powerfully to many today, with an ordered cadence that moves us lyrically from one line to another: "so draw our hearts, ... so guide our minds, so fill our imaginations, so control our wills." With each line, we open ourselves up to the transformative power of God. Like the prophet Isaiah whose mouth, whose tongue, was brought under the influence of the Divine, we respond and say, "Here am I; send me" (Isaiah 6:8).

14 In this prayer for the evening, we see a lyrical pattern similar to what is above. Here, in place of the "*so* draw ... *so* guide ... *so* ..." we have the conjunction "and" used to draw us ever further into the prayer: "*and* the evening comes, *and* the busy world is hushed, *and* the fever of life is over, *and* our work is done." When the "then" arrives, we can almost feel ourselves taking a deep breath before finishing the plea for "safe lodging, and a holy rest, and peace at the last." It is a prayer for the evening, and yet with that last phrase we see that it is simultaneously a prayer for life, culminating in heavenly rest and peace at the end of the often wearisome journey.

Direct us, O Lord, in all our doings with thy most gracious favor, and further us with thy continual help; that in all our works begun, continued, and ended in thee,[12] we may glorify thy holy Name, and finally, by thy mercy, obtain everlasting life; through Jesus Christ our Lord. Amen.

PRAYERS FOR FAMILY AND PERSONAL LIFE: #57—
FOR GUIDANCE, FROM PRAYERS AND THANKSGIVINGS

Almighty and eternal God, so draw our hearts to thee, so guide our minds, so fill our imaginations, so control our wills, that we may be wholly thine, utterly dedicated unto thee; and then use us, we pray thee, as thou wilt, and always to thy glory and the welfare of thy people; through our Lord and Savior Jesus Christ. Amen.[13]

PRAYERS FOR FAMILY AND PERSONAL LIFE: #61—
A PRAYER OF SELF-DEDICATION, FROM PRAYERS AND THANKSGIVINGS

O Lord, support us all the day long, until the shadows lengthen, and the evening comes, and the busy world is hushed, and the fever of life is over, and our work is done. Then in thy mercy, grant us a safe lodging, and a holy rest, and peace at the last. Amen.[14]

OTHER PRAYERS: #63—
IN THE EVENING, FROM PRAYERS AND THANKSGIVINGS

15 Whether he actually wrote the words or not, this prayer attributed to Francis of Assisi certainly captures the beloved saint's spirit and outlook. Notice it's not about asking God to bring peace through some heavenly miracle, but rather through us, as willing conduits of love, pardon, union, faith, hope, light, and joy. How do we accomplish this? The second part of the prayer makes it clear: we transform our thinking. As Saint Paul says in Romans 12:2, "Do not be conformed to this world, but be transformed by the renewing of your minds."

So, instead of doing the obvious, seeking to be consoled, or understood, or loved, we take a proactive, other-focused approach. We console, and understand, and love; we give, and pardon, and die to self. It is all paradoxical, but that is the heart of Jesus's message: "For those who want to save their life will lose it, and those who lose their life for my sake, and for the sake of the gospel, will save it" (Mark 8:35).

Francis lived this way, and the world around him was transformed as a result. We, too, can pray for peace and become instruments of it.

16 The Prayer Book offers several possible prayers to use at meals, what people commonly call "Grace." It is a curious thing that this is the familiar term, and yet it is appropriate, as each meal is indeed a gift, "daily bread," manna from heaven. We may speak of earning our living as being a "breadwinner," but the truth is that at any moment we could lose a job, as so many have, or if we lived in another place, faced another situation, we might find ourselves not only jobless, but homeless and hungry.

To give thanks at each meal is to affirm that it is all gift, that we are always recipients of grace. For this reason, it is right and good to have grateful hearts ... and also to be mindful of those who lack food or any essential need today.

Lord, make us instruments of your peace. Where there is hatred, let us sow love; where there is injury, pardon; where there is discord, union; where there is doubt, faith; where there is despair, hope; where there is darkness, light; where there is sadness, joy. Grant that we may not so much seek to be consoled as to console; to be understood as to understand; to be loved as to love. For it is in giving that we receive; it is in pardoning that we are pardoned; and it is in dying that we are born to eternal life. Amen.[15]

PRAYERS FOR FAMILY AND PERSONAL LIFE #62—
A PRAYER ATTRIBUTED TO ST. FRANCIS,
FROM PRAYERS AND THANKSGIVINGS

Give us grateful hearts, our Father, for all thy mercies, and make us mindful of the needs of others; through Jesus Christ our Lord. Amen.

Bless, O Lord, thy gifts to our use and us to thy service; for Christ's sake. Amen.

Blessed are you, O Lord God, King of the Universe, for you give us food to sustain our lives and make our hearts glad; through Jesus Christ our Lord. Amen.

For these and all his mercies, God's holy Name be blessed and praised; through Jesus Christ our Lord. Amen.[16]

OTHER PRAYERS: #70—
GRACE AT MEALS, FROM PRAYERS AND THANKSGIVINGS

❖ A wise soul once said that the key mark of a Christian is gratitude. Sadly, that has not always been the case, but it can be. And it should be. After all, all we have is, in some way, a gift. Hard work matters, and we do earn many things, but even the strength to do that hard work is, in the final analysis, a gift.

Yet we all too often forget this and go through life ungrateful. Some even seem to have a sense of entitlement, as if any good things that come our way are to be expected. To live this way is to miss out on so much joy. Saints see all as gift and go through life with eyes wide open, looking about to see where God is at work. Even challenges can then be seen as opportunities for greater reliance on the Divine and a more profound compassion for others around us.

This beautiful litany of thanksgiving captures so many things that we may often ignore but that truly are gifts in our lives. To take a moment and say "thank you" can be a wonderful part of a deeper spiritual life.

For the beauty and wonder of your creation, in earth and sky and sea.
We thank you, Lord.

For all that is gracious in the lives of men and women, revealing the image of Christ,
We thank you, Lord.

For our daily food and drink, our homes and families, and our friends,
We thank you, Lord.

For minds to think, and hearts to love, and hands to serve,
We thank you, Lord.

For health and strength to work, and leisure to rest and play,
We thank you, Lord.

For the brave and courageous, who are patient in suffering and faithful in adversity,
We thank you, Lord.

For all valiant seekers after truth, liberty, and justice,
We thank you, Lord.

For the communion of saints, in all times and places,
We thank you, Lord.

Above all, we give you thanks for the great mercies and promises given to us in Christ Jesus our Lord;
To him be praise and glory, with you, O Father, and the Holy Spirit, now and for ever. Amen.

GENERAL THANKSGIVING #2—

A LITANY OF THANKSGIVING, FROM PRAYERS AND THANKSGIVINGS

❖ Following the Psalter and the Prayers and Thanksgivings is the Outline of the Faith, commonly called the Catechism. Through the centuries, the question-and-answer approach to learning has allowed converts to the faith and younger members of the church to explore key Christian themes and beliefs. When certain answers lead to further, deeper discussions, all the better. This is why the Catechism lends itself so easily to small-group study or one-on-one spiritual teaching. But it can also be a useful tool to be combined with journaling, thereby creating a conversation on one's own through daily entries in the journal.

17 The Catechism is divided into several thematic sections leading from one to the next, each one including a set of questions and answers. It starts with us, with human beings, exploring what it means to be human, what it means to be part of God's created order. Other sections deal with God the Father, Jesus Christ, the Holy Spirit, the scriptures, the sacraments, and other important elements in the Christian faith and practice.

18 At one point or another in our lives, we all have asked this question, "What help is there for us?" The brief, pithy answer carries with it profound implications that can take a lifetime to explore.

19 The last answer in each section deliberately leads the reader to the next thematic section.

Human Nature
Q. What are we by nature?[17]
A. We are part of God's creation, made in the image of God.

Q. What does it mean to be created in the image of God?
A. It means that we are free to make choices: to love, to create, to reason, and to live in harmony with creation and with God.

Q. Why then do we live apart from God and out of harmony with creation?
A. From the beginning, human beings have misused their freedom and made wrong choices.

Q. Why do we not use our freedom as we should?
A. Because we rebel against God, and we put ourselves in the place of God.

Q. What help is there for us?[18]
A. Our help is in God.

Q. How did God first help us?
A. God first helped us by revealing himself and his will, through nature and history, through many seers and saints, and especially through the prophets of Israel.[19]

AN OUTLINE OF THE FAITH, OR CATECHISM

❖ Between the Catechism and the lectionaries that compose the final part of the BCP, there are a few collected writings from the church's heritage in the section known as Historical Documents. Among the items found there is the Chicago-Lambeth Quadrilateral, so named because it was born out of the House of Bishops of the Episcopal Church meeting in Chicago, then confirmed with some minor revisions by the bishops of the Anglican Communion meeting at Lambeth Palace. It then also went on to be ratified by the Episcopal Church's House of Deputies.

20 The Quadrilateral was designed to provide the basis for Christian reunion, offering the bottom line, as it were, of what is required for Episcopalians and Anglicans to explore issues of partnership and communion with other Christian traditions. The four points speak of our commitment to Word, Creed, Sacrament, and the Historic Episcopate.

21 Anglicans, like Roman Catholics and unlike most Protestants, include in our Bibles those additional books known as the Apocrypha. But in terms of conversations toward reunion, our bare minimum is the Hebrew and Christian scriptures.

22 While we speak of other sacramental rites such as Matrimony and Orders, these two gospel sacraments constitute our bottom line, as it were.

23 This remains a difficult point for denominations that have not traditionally held up the importance of the apostolic succession.

The following Articles supply a basis on which approach may be by God's blessing made towards Home Reunion:[20]

(a) The Holy Scriptures of the Old and New Testaments, as "containing all things necessary to salvation," and as being the rule and ultimate standard of faith.[21]

(b) The Apostles' Creed, as the Baptismal Symbol; and the Nicene Creed, as the sufficient statement of the Christian faith.

(c) The two Sacraments ordained by Christ Himself—Baptism and the Supper of the Lord—ministered with unfailing use of Christ's words of Institution, and of the elements ordained by Him.[22]

(d) The Historic Episcopate, locally adapted in the methods of its administration to the varying needs of the nations and peoples called of God into the Unity of His Church.[23]

LAMBETH CONFERENCE OF 1888, RESOLUTION II,
FROM THE CHICAGO-LAMBETH QUADRILATERAL 1886, 1888

Using the Prayer Book as a Spiritual Tool ☐

We have seen some of the precious gems that are in this treasure chest called the Prayer Book. But aside from pulling out a prayer here or a prayer there, how can you actually use the book in your daily life as a spiritual tool, a helpful resource that you can use not just sporadically, but regularly and systematically?

The answer lies in the Prayer Book itself. As we have seen, after the initial introductory pages, the BCP moves into a large section known as the Daily Office. Here we find the monastic tradition of Anglicanism as a gift to us in our own devotional life. We find there sets of prayers for both the morning and the evening, set in both contemporary and traditional English. There are also two additional forms for prayer at noon and the close of the day. Although this is a gift from the monks of old, we do not have to be monks or nuns today to use these prayer forms. Indeed, it is interesting to see today a desire on the part of many for a tool to help in reading through the Scriptures in a regularized way, perhaps over a year. With the Daily Office, we see a longstanding tradition of this kind of devotion for use by us.

So what can you do with it?

First, this may seem obvious, but the first step is to buy a Book of Common Prayer. This study has focused on the 1979 BCP, but hopefully has also shown that there are alternatives as well. Even if we talk about the 1979 Prayer Book, we have some choices: large-print editions, beau-tiful leather-bound editions, pocket-sized editions, combination editions that include the Bible or hymnal.

Second, set aside time each day—a regular, consistent time that you know will not change from day to day. Depending on the time you choose, you can then use the corresponding prayer service from the Daily Office, whether for the morning or evening or end of day.

Third, it is important to find a place for this time of prayer. All the world belongs to God, but we do take note of sacred spaces, those places that we set apart for devotional use. For you, it can be a church sanctuary, but it can also be a particular space in the home that is set apart for your devotional time, much like a spiritual "time-sharing."

Fourth, use the service that you have chosen, and use it in a regularized fashion day after day. This is difficult for some, who like to argue that spontaneous prayer is best. The beauty of the Daily Office is that the structure allows for spontaneity. But the structure is important because we are creatures of habits and patterns, and part of the gift of the Daily Office is that it can give us a new pattern, a new habit. If you make a commitment to this over a one-month period, then you can refine the pattern to fit what you need, but you will indeed now have a pattern of prayer.

Fifth, because the Daily Office also includes a regularized format for reading scripture, this is where you turn from the front of the Prayer Book to the back, to the Daily Office Lectionary. Unlike the corresponding Eucharistic Lectionary, which is divided into three years (A, B, and C) with chosen passages that are read each Sunday, the Daily Office Lectionary is set up for a two-year, fully comprehensive reading of the entire Bible. This is where spiritual discipline is needed, as there will be large sections of scripture that seem a tad ... boring. It might seem like it takes an eternity to work through the genealogy lists of Numbers and the ritual laws of Leviticus, but these are parts of a larger whole.

Sixth, move beyond the Daily Office and Lectionary and begin to familiarize yourself with the rest of the Prayer Book. Then you can consider how some of the various sections and services therein can be of help to you at key moments in your life. As this book has attempted to show, there are so many ways to use sections of the BCP that may not at first seem to be relevant.

In all of this, it should be reiterated that it is a book of common prayer and therefore must be understood first and foremost as the primary liturgical tool of Episcopal and Anglican congregations. The Prayer Book is most genuinely itself when it is used in a faith community. Having said that, however, I hope that this study has given a glimpse of the inestimable value of this spiritual treasure chest, not just for a community but for an individual, not just for Episcopalians and Anglicans, but for seekers and spiritual pilgrims of all sorts and varieties.

In the end, the Prayer Book is not only our book, not only Cranmer's book, not only the church's book. It is also your book. So read it, make use of it, enjoy it, and be blessed by it.

Suggestions for Further Reading ☐

DeSilva, David A. *Sacramental Life: Spiritual Formation Through the Book of Common Prayer.* Downers Grove, IL: IVP Books, 2008.

Earle, Mary C. *Celtic Christian Spirituality: Essential Writings—Annotated and Explained.* Woodstock, VT: SkyLight Paths, 2011.

Hatchett, Marion J. *Commentary on the American Prayer Book.* New York: HarperCollins, 1995.

Jefferts Schori, Katharine. *Gathering at God's Table: The Meaning of Mission in the Feast of Faith.* Woodstock, VT: SkyLight Paths, 2012.

Lee, Jeffrey. *Opening the Prayer Book.* Lanham, MD: Cowley Publications, 1999.

Markham, Ian S., *Liturgical Life Principles.* New York: Morehouse, 2009.

Markham, Ian S., and C. K. Robertson. *Episcopal Questions, Episcopal Answers.* New York: Church Publishing, 2014.

Price, Charles P., and Louis Weil. *Liturgy for Living*, rev. ed. New York: Morehouse, 2000.

Robertson, C. K. *A Dangerous Dozen: 12 Christians Who Threatened the Status Quo but Taught Us to Live Like Jesus.* Woodstock, VT: SkyLight Paths, 2011.

Inspiration

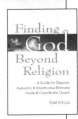

Finding God Beyond Religion: A Guide for Skeptics, Agnostics & Unorthodox Believers Inside & Outside the Church
By Tom Stella; Foreword by The Rev. Canon Marianne Wells Borg
Reinterprets traditional religious teachings central to the Christian faith for people who have outgrown the beliefs and devotional practices that once made sense to them.
6 x 9, 160 pp, Quality PB, 978-1-59473-485-4 **$16.99**

How Did I Get to Be 70 When I'm 35 Inside?: Spiritual Surprises of Later Life *By Linda Douty*
Encourages you to focus on the inner changes of aging to help you greet your later years as the grand adventure they can be. 6 x 9, 208 pp, Quality PB, 978-1-59473-297-3 **$16.99**

Fully Awake and Truly Alive: Spiritual Practices to Nurture Your Soul
By Rev. Jane E. Vennard; Foreword by Rami Shapiro
Illustrates the joys and frustrations of spiritual practice, offers insights from various religious traditions and provides exercises and meditations to help us become more fully alive.
6 x 9, 208 pp, Quality PB, 978-1-59473-473-1 **$16.99**

Saving Civility: 52 Ways to Tame Rude, Crude & Attitude for a Polite Planet
By Sara Hacala
Provides fifty-two practical ways you can reverse the course of incivility and make the world a more enriching, pleasant place to live.
6 x 9, 240 pp, Quality PB 978-1-59473-314-7 **$16.99**

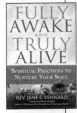

Spiritually Healthy Divorce: Navigating Disruption with Insight & Hope
By Carolyne Call
A spiritual map to help you move through the twists and turns of divorce.
6 x 9, 224 pp, Quality PB, 978-1-59473-288-1 **$16.99**

Who Is My God? 2nd Edition
An Innovative Guide to Finding Your Spiritual Identity
By the Editors at SkyLight Paths
Provides the Spiritual Identity Self-Test™ to uncover the components of your unique spirituality. 6 x 9, 160 pp, Quality PB, 978-1-59473-014-6 **$15.99**

Journeys of Simplicity
Traveling Light with Thomas Merton, Bashō,
Edward Abbey, Annie Dillard & Others
By Philip Harnden
Invites you to consider a more graceful way of traveling through life.
PB includes journal pages to help you get started on
your own spiritual journey.
5 x 7¼, 144 pp, Quality PB, 978-1-59473-181-5 **$12.99**
5 x 7¼, 128 pp, HC, 978-1-893361-76-8 **$16.95**

Or phone, fax, mail or e-mail to: SKYLIGHT PATHS Publishing
Sunset Farm Offices, Route 4 • P.O. Box 237 • Woodstock, Vermont 05091
Tel: (802) 457-4000 • Fax: (802) 457-4004 • www.skylightpaths.com
Credit card orders: (800) 962-4544 (8:30AM–5:30PM EST Monday–Friday)
Generous discounts on quantity orders. SATISFACTION GUARANTEED. Prices subject to change.

Bible Stories / Folktales

Abraham's Bind & Other Bible Tales of Trickery, Folly, Mercy and Love By Michael J. Caduto
New retellings of episodes in the lives of familiar biblical characters explore relevant life lessons. 6 x 9, 224 pp, HC, 978-1-59473-186-0 **$19.99**

Daughters of the Desert: Stories of Remarkable Women from Christian, Jewish and Muslim Traditions By Claire Rudolf Murphy,
Meghan Nuttall Sayres, Mary Cronk Farrell, Sarah Conover and Betsy Wharton
Breathes new life into the old tales of our female ancestors in faith. Uses traditional scriptural passages as starting points, then with vivid detail fills in historical context and place. Chapters reveal the voices of Sarah, Hagar, Huldah, Esther, Salome, Mary Magdalene, Lydia, Khadija, Fatima and many more. Historical fiction ideal for readers of all ages.
5½ x 8½, 192 pp, Quality PB, 978-1-59473-106-8 **$14.99** Inc. reader's discussion guide

The Triumph of Eve & Other Subversive Bible Tales
By Matt Biers-Ariel
These engaging retellings of familiar Bible stories are witty, often hilarious and always profound. They invite you to grapple with questions and issues that are often hidden in the original texts.
5½ x 8½, 192 pp, Quality PB, 978-1-59473-176-1 **$14.99**

Also available: The Triumph of Eve Teacher's Guide
8½ x 11, 44 pp, PB, 978-1-59473-152-5 **$8.99**

Wisdom in the Telling
Finding Inspiration and Grace in Traditional Folktales and Myths Retold
By Lorraine Hartin-Gelardi
6 x 9, 192 pp, HC, 978-1-59473-185-3 **$19.99**

Religious Etiquette / Reference

How to Be a Perfect Stranger, 5th Edition: The Essential Religious Etiquette Handbook Edited by Stuart M. Matlins and Arthur J. Magida
The indispensable guidebook to help the well-meaning guest when visiting other people's religious ceremonies. A straightforward guide to the rituals and celebrations of the major religions and denominations in the United States and Canada from the perspective of an interested guest of any other faith, based on information obtained from authorities of each religion. Belongs in every living room, library and office. Covers:

African American Methodist Churches • Assemblies of God • Bahá'í Faith • Baptist • Buddhist • Christian Church (Disciples of Christ) • Christian Science (Church of Christ, Scientist) • Churches of Christ • Episcopalian and Anglican • Hindu • Islam • Jehovah's Witnesses • Jewish • Lutheran • Mennonite/Amish • Methodist • Mormon (Church of Jesus Christ of Latter-day Saints) • Native American/First Nations • Orthodox Churches • Pentecostal Church of God • Presbyterian • Quaker (Religious Society of Friends) • Reformed Church in America/Canada • Roman Catholic • Seventh-day Adventist • Sikh • Unitarian Universalist • United Church of Canada • United Church of Christ

"The things Miss Manners forgot to tell us about religion."
—*Los Angeles Times*

"Finally, for those inclined to undertake their own spiritual journeys ... tells visitors what to expect." —*New York Times*

6 x 9, 432 pp, Quality PB, 978-1-59473-294-2 **$19.99**

The Perfect Stranger's Guide to Funerals and Grieving Practices: A Guide to Etiquette in Other People's Religious Ceremonies Edited by Stuart M. Matlins
6 x 9, 240 pp, Quality PB, 978-1-893361-20-1 **$16.95**

The Perfect Stranger's Guide to Wedding Ceremonies: A Guide to Etiquette in Other People's Religious Ceremonies Edited by Stuart M. Matlins
6 x 9, 208 pp, Quality PB, 978-1-893361-19-5 **$16.95**

Sacred Texts—SkyLight Illuminations Series

Offers today's spiritual seeker an enjoyable entry into the great classic texts of the world's spiritual traditions. Each classic is presented in an accessible translation, with facing pages of guided commentary from experts, giving you the keys you need to understand the history, context and meaning of the text.

CHRISTIANITY

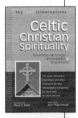

Celtic Christian Spirituality: Essential Writings—Annotated & Explained
Annotation by Mary C. Earle; Foreword by John Philip Newell
Explores how the writings of this lively tradition embody the gospel.
5½ x 8½, 176 pp, Quality PB, 978-1-59473-302-4 **$16.99**

Desert Fathers and Mothers: Early Christian Wisdom Sayings—
Annotated & Explained *Annotation by Christine Valters Paintner, PhD*
Opens up wisdom of the desert fathers and mothers for readers with no previous knowledge of Western monasticism and early Christianity.
5½ x 8½, 192 pp, Quality PB, 978-1-59473-373-4 **$16.99**

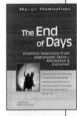

The End of Days: Essential Selections from Apocalyptic Texts—
Annotated & Explained *Annotation by Robert G. Clouse, PhD*
Helps you understand the complex Christian visions of the end of the world.
5½ x 8½, 224 pp, Quality PB, 978-1-59473-170-9 **$16.99**

The Hidden Gospel of Matthew: Annotated & Explained
Translation & Annotation by Ron Miller
Discover the words and events that have the strongest connection to the historical Jesus.
5½ x 8½, 272 pp, Quality PB, 978-1-59473-038-2 **$16.99**

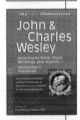

The Imitation of Christ: Selections Annotated & Explained
Annotation by Paul Wesley Chilcote, PhD; By Thomas à Kempis; Adapted from John Wesley's
The Christian's Pattern
Let Jesus's example of holiness, humility and purity of heart be a companion on your own spiritual journey.
5½ x 8½, 224 pp, Quality PB, 978-1-59473-434-2 **$16.99**

The Infancy Gospels of Jesus: Apocryphal Tales from the Childhoods of Mary and Jesus—Annotated & Explained
Translation & Annotation by Stevan Davies; Foreword by A. Edward Siecienski, PhD
A startling presentation of the early lives of Mary, Jesus and other biblical figures that will amuse and surprise you.
5½ x 8½, 176 pp, Quality PB, 978-1-59473-258-4 **$16.99**

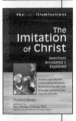

John & Charles Wesley: Selections from Their Writings and Hymns—
Annotated & Explained
Annotation by Paul W. Chilcote, PhD
A unique presentation of the writings of these two inspiring brothers brings together some of the most essential material from their large corpus of work.
5½ x 8½, 288 pp, Quality PB, 978-1-59473-309-3 **$16.99**

The Lost Sayings of Jesus: Teachings from Ancient Christian, Jewish, Gnostic and Islamic Sources—Annotated & Explained
Translation & Annotation by Andrew Phillip Smith; Foreword by Stephan A. Hoeller
This collection of more than three hundred sayings depicts Jesus as a Wisdom teacher who speaks to people of all faiths as a mystic and spiritual master.
5½ x 8½, 240 pp, Quality PB, 978-1-59473-172-3 **$16.99**

Philokalia: The Eastern Christian Spiritual Texts—Selections
Annotated & Explained *Annotation by Allyne Smith; Translation by G. E. H. Palmer,*
Phillip Sherrard and Bishop Kallistos Ware
The first approachable introduction to the wisdom of the Philokalia, the classic text of Eastern Christian spirituality.
5½ x 8½, 240 pp, Quality PB, 978-1-59473-103-7 **$16.99**

Sacred Texts—continued

CHRISTIANITY—continued

The Sacred Writings of Paul: Selections Annotated & Explained
Translation & Annotation by Ron Miller
Leads you into the exciting immediacy of Paul's teachings.
5½ x 8½, 224 pp, Quality PB, 978-1-59473-213-3 **$16.99**

Saint Augustine of Hippo: Selections from *Confessions* and Other
Essential Writings—Annotated & Explained
Annotation by Joseph T. Kelley, PhD; Translation by the Augustinian Heritage Institute
Provides insight into the mind and heart of this foundational Christian figure.
5½ x 8½, 272 pp, Quality PB, 978-1-59473-282-9 **$16.99**

Saint Ignatius Loyola—The Spiritual Writings: Selections
Annotated & Explained *Annotation by Mark Mossa, SJ*
Draws from contemporary translations of original texts focusing on the practical
mysticism of Ignatius of Loyola.
5½ x 8½, 288 pp, Quality PB, 978-1-59473-301-7 **$16.99**

Sex Texts from the Bible: Selections Annotated & Explained
Translation & Annotation by Teresa J. Hornsby; Foreword by Amy-Jill Levine
Demystifies the Bible's ideas on gender roles, marriage, sexual orientation, virginity,
lust and sexual pleasure.
5½ x 8½, 208 pp, Quality PB, 978-1-59473-217-1 **$16.99**

Spiritual Writings on Mary: Annotated & Explained
Annotation by Mary Ford-Grabowsky; Foreword by Andrew Harvey
Examines the role of Mary, the mother of Jesus, as a source of inspiration in history and in life today.
5½ x 8½, 288 pp, Quality PB, 978-1-59473-001-6 **$16.99**

The Way of a Pilgrim: The Jesus Prayer Journey—Annotated &
Explained
Translation & Annotation by Gleb Pokrovsky; Foreword by Andrew Harvey
A classic of Russian Orthodox spirituality.
5½ x 8½, 160 pp, Illus., Quality PB, 978-1-893361-31-7 **$14.95**

GNOSTICISM

Gnostic Writings on the Soul: Annotated & Explained
Translation & Annotation by Andrew Phillip Smith; Foreword by Stephan A. Hoeller
Reveals the inspiring ways your soul can remember and return to its unique,
divine purpose.
5½ x 8½, 144 pp, Quality PB, 978-1-59473-220-1 **$16.99**

The Gospel of Philip: Annotated & Explained
Translation & Annotation by Andrew Phillip Smith; Foreword by Stevan Davies
Reveals otherwise unrecorded sayings of Jesus and fragments of Gnostic mythology.
5½ x 8½, 160 pp, Quality PB, 978-1-59473-111-2 **$16.99**

The Gospel of Thomas: Annotated & Explained
Translation & Annotation by Stevan Davies; Foreword by Andrew Harvey
Sheds new light on the origins of Christianity and portrays Jesus as a wisdom-loving sage.
5½ x 8½, 192 pp, Quality PB, 978-1-893361-45-4 **$16.99**

The Secret Book of John: The Gnostic Gospel—Annotated & Explained
Translation & Annotation by Stevan Davies
The most significant and influential text of the ancient Gnostic religion.
5½ x 8½, 208 pp, Quality PB, 978-1-59473-082-5 **$16.99**

Sacred Texts—continued

JUDAISM

The Book of Job: Annotated & Explained
Translation and Annotation by Donald Kraus; Foreword by Dr. Marc Brettler
Clarifies for today's readers what Job is, how to overcome difficulties in the text, and what it may mean for us.
5½ x 8½, 256 pp, Quality PB, 978-1-59473-389-5 **$16.99**

The Divine Feminine in Biblical Wisdom Literature
Selections Annotated & Explained
Translation & Annotation by Rabbi Rami Shapiro; Foreword by Rev. Cynthia Bourgeault, PhD
Uses the Hebrew Bible and Wisdom literature to explain Sophia's way of wisdom and illustrate Her creative energy.
5½ x 8½, 240 pp, Quality PB, 978-1-59473-109-9 **$16.99**

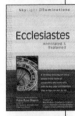

Ecclesiastes: Annotated & Explained
Translation and Annotation by Rabbi Rami Shapiro; Foreword by Rev. Barbara Cawthorne Crafton
A timeless teaching on living well amid uncertainty and insecurity.
5½ x 8¼, 160 pp, Quality PB, 978-1-59473-287-4 **$16.99**

Ethics of the Sages: *Pirke Avot*—Annotated & Explained
Translation & Annotation by Rabbi Rami Shapiro
Clarifies the ethical teachings of the early Rabbis.
5½ x 8¼, 192 pp, Quality PB, 978-1-59473-207-2 **$16.99**

Hasidic Tales: Annotated & Explained
Translation & Annotation by Rabbi Rami Shapiro; Foreword by Andrew Harvey
Introduces the legendary tales of the impassioned Hasidic rabbis, presenting them as stories rather than as parables.
5½ x 8¼, 240 pp, Quality PB, 978-1-893361-86-7 **$16.95**

The Hebrew Prophets: Selections Annotated & Explained
Translation & Annotation by Rabbi Rami Shapiro;
Foreword by Rabbi Zalman M. Schachter-Shalomi
5½ x 8¼, 224 pp, Quality PB, 978-1-59473-037-5 **$16.99**

Maimonides—Essential Teachings on Jewish Faith & Ethics
The Book of Knowledge & the Thirteen Principles of Faith—Annotated & Explained
Translation and Annotation by Rabbi Marc D. Angel, PhD
Opens up for us Maimonides's views on the nature of God, providence, prophecy, free will, human nature, repentance and more.
5½ x 8½, 224 pp, Quality PB, 978-1-59473-311-6 **$18.99**

Proverbs: Annotated & Explained
Translation and Annotation by Rabbi Rami Shapiro
Demonstrates how these complex poetic forms are actually straightforward instructions to live simply, without rationalizations and excuses.
5½ x 8½, 288 pp, Quality PB, 978-1-59473-310-9 $16.99

Tanya, the Masterpiece of Hasidic Wisdom
Selections Annotated & Explained
Translation & Annotation by Rabbi Rami Shapiro; Foreword by Rabbi Zalman M. Schachter-Shalomi
Clarifies one of the most powerful and potentially transformative books of Jewish wisdom.
5½ x 8¼, 240 pp, Quality PB, 978-1-59473-275-1 **$16.99**

Zohar: Annotated & Explained
Translation & Annotation by Daniel C. Matt; Foreword by Andrew Harvey
The canonical text of Jewish mystical tradition.
5½ x 8¼, 176 pp, Quality PB, 978-1-893361-51-5 **$16.99**

Sacred Texts—continued

ISLAM

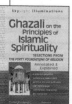

Ghazali on the Principles of Islamic Spirituality

Selections from *The Forty Foundations of Religion*—Annotated & Explained
Translation & Annotation by Aaron Spevack, PhD
Makes the core message of this influential spiritual master relevant to anyone seeking a balanced understanding of Islam.
5½ x 8½, 338 pp, Quality PB, 978-1-59473-284-3 **$18.99**

The Qur'an and Sayings of Prophet Muhammad

Selections Annotated & Explained
Annotation by Sohaib N. Sultan; Translation by Yusuf Ali, Revised by Sohaib N. Sultan; Foreword by Jane I. Smith
Presents the foundational wisdom of Islam in an easy-to-use format.
5½ x 8½, 256 pp, Quality PB, 978-1-59473-222-5 **$16.99**

Rumi and Islam: Selections from His Stories, Poems, and Discourses—

Annotated & Explained *Translation & Annotation by Ibrahim Gamard*
Focuses on Rumi's place within the Sufi tradition of Islam, providing insight into the mystical side of the religion.
5½ x 8½, 240 pp, Quality PB, 978-1-59473-002-3 **$15.99**

EASTERN RELIGIONS

The Art of War—Spirituality for Conflict: Annotated & Explained

By Sun Tzu; Annotation by Thomas Huynh; Translation by Thomas Huynh and the Editors at Sonshi.com; Foreword by Marc Benioff; Preface by Thomas Cleary
Highlights principles that encourage a perceptive and spiritual approach to conflict.
5½ x 8½, 256 pp, Quality PB, 978-1-59473-244-7 **$16.99**

Bhagavad Gita: Annotated & Explained

Translation by Shri Purohit Swami; Annotation by Kendra Crossen Burroughs; Foreword by Andrew Harvey
Presents the classic text's teachings—with no previous knowledge of Hinduism required.
5½ x 8½, 192 pp, Quality PB, 978-1-893361-28-7 **$16.95**

Chuang-tzu: The Tao of Perfect Happiness—Selections Annotated & Explained

Translation & Annotation by Livia Kohn, PhD
Presents Taoism's central message of reverence for the "Way" of the natural world.
5½ x 8½, 240 pp, Quality PB, 978-1-59473-296-6 **$16.99**

Confucius, the *Analects:* The Path of the Sage—Selections Annotated

& Explained *Annotation by Rodney L. Taylor, PhD; Translation by James Legge, Revised by Rodney L. Taylor, PhD* Explores the ethical and spiritual meaning behind the Confucian way of learning and self-cultivation.
5½ x 8½, 192 pp, Quality PB, 978-1-59473-306-2 **$16.99**

Dhammapada: Annotated & Explained

Translation by Max Müller, revised by Jack Maguire; Annotation by Jack Maguire; Foreword by Andrew Harvey Contains all of Buddhism's key teachings, plus commentary that explains all the names, terms and references.
5½ x 8½, 160 pp, b/w photos, Quality PB, 978-1-893361-42-3 **$14.95**

Selections from the Gospel of Sri Ramakrishna: Annotated & Explained

Translation by Swami Nikhilananda; Annotation by Kendra Crossen Burroughs; Foreword by Andrew Harvey Introduces the fascinating world of the Indian mystic and the universal appeal of his message.
5½ x 8½, 240 pp, b/w photos, Quality PB, 978-1-893361-46-1 **$16.95**

Tao Te Ching: Annotated & Explained

Translation & Annotation by Derek Lin; Foreword by Lama Surya Das
Introduces an Eastern classic in an accessible, poetic and completely original way.
5½ x 8½, 208 pp, Quality PB, 978-1-59473-204-1 **$16.99**

Children's Spirituality

Remembering My Grandparent: A Kid's Own Grief Workbook
in the Christian Tradition *By Nechama Liss-Levinson, PhD, and Rev. Molly Phinney Baskette, MDiv* 8 x 10, 48 pp, 2-color text, HC, 978-1-59473-212-6 **$16.99** *For ages 7 & up*

Does God Ever Sleep? *By Joan Sauro, CSJ*
A charming nighttime reminder that God is always present in our lives.
10 x 8¼, 32 pp, Full-color photos, Quality PB, 978-1-59473-110-5 **$8.99** *For ages 3–6*

Does God Forgive Me? *By August Gold; Full-color photos by Diane Hardy Waller*
Gently shows how God forgives all that we do if we are truly sorry.
10 x 8¼, 32 pp, Full-color photos, Quality PB, 978-1-59473-142-6 **$8.99** *For ages 3–6*

God Said Amen *By Sandy Eisenberg Sasso; Full-color illus. by Avi Katz*
A warm and inspiring tale that shows us that we need only reach out to
each other to find the answers to our prayers.
9 x 12, 32 pp, Full-color illus., HC, 978-1-58023-080-3 **$16.95*** *For ages 4 & up*

How Does God Listen? *By Kay Lindahl; Full-color photos by Cynthia Maloney*
How do we know when God is listening to us? Children will find the
answers to these questions as they engage their senses while the story
unfolds, learning how God listens in the wind, waves, clouds, hot chocolate, perfume, our tears and our laughter.
10 x 8¼, 32 pp, Full-color photos, Quality PB, 978-1-59473-084-9 **$8.99** *For ages 3–6*

In God's Hands *By Lawrence Kushner and Gary Schmidt; Full-color illus. by Matthew J. Baek*
A delightful, timeless legend that tells of the ordinary miracles that occur when
we really, truly open our eyes to the world around us.
9 x 12, 32 pp, Full-color illus., HC, 978-1-58023-224-1 **$16.99*** *For ages 5 & up*

In God's Name *By Sandy Eisenberg Sasso; Full-color illus. by Phoebe Stone*
Like an ancient myth in its poetic text and vibrant illustrations, this award-winning
modern fable about the search for God's name celebrates the diversity and, at the
same time, the unity of all the people of the world.
9 x 12, 32 pp, Full-color illus., HC, 978-1-879045-26-2 **$16.99*** *For ages 4 & up*

Also available in Spanish: **El nombre de Dios**
9 x 12, 32 pp, Full-color illus., HC, 978-1-893361-63-8 **$16.95**

In Our Image: God's First Creatures
By Nancy Sohn Swartz; Full-color illus. by Melanie Hall
A playful new twist on the Genesis story—from the perspective of the animals.
Celebrates the interconnectedness of nature and the harmony of all living things.
9 x 12, 32 pp, Full-color illus., HC, 978-1-879045-99-6 **$16.95*** *For ages 4 & up*

Noah's Wife: The Story of Naamah
By Sandy Eisenberg Sasso; Full-color illus. by Bethanne Andersen
Opens young readers' religious imaginations to new ideas about the well-known
story of the Flood. When God tells Noah to bring the animals of the world onto
the ark, God also calls on Naamah, Noah's wife, to save each plant on Earth.
9 x 12, 32 pp, Full-color illus., HC, 978-1-58023-134-3 **$16.95*** *For ages 4 & up*

Also available: **Naamah:** Noah's Wife (A Board Book)
By Sandy Eisenberg Sasso; Full-color illus. by Bethanne Andersen
5 x 5, 24 pp, Full-color illus., Board Book, 978-1-893361-56-0 **$7.95** *For ages 0–4*

Where Does God Live? *By August Gold and Matthew J. Perlman*
Helps children and their parents find God in the world around us with
simple, practical examples children can relate to.
10 x 8¼, 32 pp, Full-color photos, Quality PB, 978-1-893361-39-3 **$8.99** *For ages 3–6*

* A book from Jewish Lights, SkyLight Paths' sister imprint

Spirituality & Crafts

Beading—The Creative Spirit: Finding Your Sacred Center through the Art of Beadwork *By Rev. Wendy Ellsworth*
Invites you on a spiritual pilgrimage into the kaleidoscope world of glass and color. 7 x 9, 240 pp, 8-page color insert, 40+ b/w photos and 40 diagrams,
Quality PB, 978-1-59473-267-6 **$18.99**

Contemplative Crochet: A Hands-On Guide for Interlocking Faith and Craft *By Cindy Crandall-Frazier; Foreword by Linda Skolnik*
Illuminates the spiritual lessons you can learn through crocheting.
7 x 9, 208 pp, b/w photos, Quality PB, 978-1-59473-238-6 **$16.99**

The Knitting Way: A Guide to Spiritual Self-Discovery
By Linda Skolnik and Janice MacDaniels Examines how you can explore and strengthen your spiritual life through knitting.
7 x 9, 240 pp, b/w photos, Quality PB, 978-1-59473-079-5 **$16.99**

The Painting Path: Embodying Spiritual Discovery through Yoga, Brush and Color *By Linda Novick; Foreword by Richard Segalman*
Explores the divine connection you can experience through art.
7 x 9, 208 pp, 8-page color insert, plus b/w photos,
Quality PB, 978-1-59473-226-3 **$18.99**

The Quilting Path: A Guide to Spiritual Discovery through Fabric, Thread and Kabbalah *By Louise Silk*
Explores how to cultivate personal growth through quilt making.
7 x 9, 192 pp, b/w photos and illus., Quality PB, 978-1-59473-206-5 **$16.99**

The Scrapbooking Journey: A Hands-On Guide to Spiritual Discovery
By Cory Richardson-Lauve; Foreword by Stacy Julian Reveals how this craft can become a practice used to deepen and shape your life.
7 x 9, 176 pp, 8-page color insert, plus b/w photos, Quality PB, 978-1-59473-216-4 **$18.99**

The Soulwork of Clay: A Hands-On Approach to Spirituality
By Marjory Zoet Bankson; Photos by Peter Bankson
Takes you through the seven-step process of making clay into a pot, drawing parallels at each stage to the process of spiritual growth.
7 x 9, 192 pp, b/w photos, Quality PB, 978-1-59473-249-2 **$16.99**

Kabbalah / Enneagram
(Books from Jewish Lights Publishing, SkyLight Paths' sister imprint)

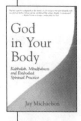

Cast in God's Image: Discover Your Personality Type Using the Enneagram and Kabbalah
By Rabbi Howard A. Addison, PhD 7 x 9, 176 pp, Quality PB, 978-1-58023-124-4 **$16.95**

Ehyeh: A Kabbalah for Tomorrow *By Rabbi Arthur Green, PhD*
6 x 9, 224 pp, Quality PB, 978-1-58023-213-5 **$18.99**

The Enneagram and Kabbalah, 2nd Edition: Reading Your Soul
By Rabbi Howard A. Addison, PhD 6 x 9, 192 pp, Quality PB, 978-1-58023-229-6 **$16.99**

The Gift of Kabbalah: Discovering the Secrets of Heaven, Renewing Your Life on Earth
By Tamar Frankiel, PhD 6 x 9, 256 pp, Quality PB, 978-1-58023-141-1 **$16.95**

God in Your Body: Kabbalah, Mindfulness and Embodied Spiritual Practice
By Jay Michaelson 6 x 9, 272 pp, Quality PB, 978-1-58023-304-0 **$18.99**

Jewish Mysticism and the Spiritual Life: Classical Texts, Contemporary Reflections
Edited by Dr. Lawrence Fine, Dr. Eitan Fishbane and Rabbi Or N. Rose
6 x 9, 256 pp, HC, 978-1-58023-434-4 **$24.99**

Kabbalah: A Brief Introduction for Christians
By Tamar Frankiel, PhD 5½ x 8½, 208 pp, Quality PB, 978-1-58023-303-3 **$16.99**

Zohar: Annotated & Explained *Translation & Annotation by Daniel C. Matt;*
Foreword by Andrew Harvey 5½ x 8½, 176 pp, Quality PB, 978-1-893361-51-5 **$15.99**

Women's Interest

Birthing God: Women's Experiences of the Divine
By Lana Dalberg; Foreword by Kathe Schaaf
Powerful narratives of suffering, love and hope that inspire both personal and collective transformation. 6 x 9, 304 pp, Quality PB, 978-1-59473-480-9 **$18.99**

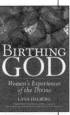

On the Chocolate Trail: A Delicious Adventure Connecting Jews, Religions, History, Travel, Rituals and Recipes to the Magic of Cacao
By Rabbi Deborah R. Prinz
Take a delectable journey through the religious history of chocolate—a real treat!
6 x 9, 272 pp, 20+ b/w photographs, Quality PB, 978-1-58023-487-0 **$18.99***

Women, Spirituality and Transformative Leadership
Where Grace Meets Power
Edited by Kathe Schaaf, Kay Lindahl, Kathleen S. Hurty, PhD, and Reverend Guo Cheen
A dynamic conversation on the power of women's spiritual leadership and its emerging patterns of transformation. 6 x 9, 288 pp, HC, 978-1-59473-313-0 **$24.99**

Spiritually Healthy Divorce: Navigating Disruption with Insight & Hope
By Carolyne Call A spiritual map to help you move through the twists and turns of divorce. 6 x 9, 224 pp, Quality PB, 978-1-59473-288-1 **$16.99**

New Feminist Christianity: Many Voices, Many Views
Edited by Mary E. Hunt and Diann L. Neu
Insights from ministers and theologians, activists and leaders, artists and liturgists who are shaping the future. Taken together, their voices offer a starting point for building new models of religious life and worship.
6 x 9, 384 pp, Quality PB, 978-1-59473-435-9 **$19.99**; HC, 978-1-59473-285-0 **$24.99**

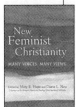

Bread, Body, Spirit: Finding the Sacred in Food
Edited and with Introductions by Alice Peck 6 x 9, 224 pp, Quality PB, 978-1-59473-242-3 **$19.99**

Dance—The Sacred Art: The Joy of Movement as a Spiritual Practice
By Cynthia Winton-Henry 5½ x 8½, 224 pp, Quality PB, 978-1-59473-268-3 **$16.99**

Daughters of the Desert: Stories of Remarkable Women from Christian, Jewish and Muslim Traditions
By Claire Rudolf Murphy, Meghan Nuttall Sayres, Mary Cronk Farrell, Sarah Conover and Betsy Wharton
5½ x 8½, 192 pp, Illus., Quality PB, 978-1-59473-106-8 **$14.99** Inc. reader's discussion guide

The Divine Feminine in Biblical Wisdom Literature
Selections Annotated & Explained
Translation & Annotation by Rabbi Rami Shapiro; Foreword by Rev. Cynthia Bourgeault, PhD
5½ x 8½, 240 pp, Quality PB, 978-1-59473-109-9 **$16.99**

Divining the Body: Reclaim the Holiness of Your Physical Self
By Jan Phillips 8 x 8, 256 pp, Quality PB, 978-1-59473-080-1 **$18.99**

Honoring Motherhood: Prayers, Ceremonies & Blessings
Edited and with Introductions by Lynn L. Caruso
5 x 7¼, 272 pp, Quality PB, 978-1-58473-384-0 **$9.99**; HC, 978-1-59473-239-3 **$19.99**

Next to Godliness: Finding the Sacred in Housekeeping
Edited by Alice Peck 6 x 9, 224 pp, Quality PB, 978-1-59473-214-0 **$19.99**

ReVisions: Seeing Torah through a Feminist Lens
By Rabbi Elyse Goldstein 5½ x 8½, 224 pp, Quality PB, 978-1-58023-117-6 **$16.95***

The Triumph of Eve & Other Subversive Bible Tales
By Matt Biers-Ariel 5½ x 8½, 192 pp, Quality PB, 978-1-59473-176-1 **$14.99**

White Fire: A Portrait of Women Spiritual Leaders in America
By Malka Drucker; Photos by Gay Block 7 x 10, 320 pp, b/w photos, HC, 978-1-893361-64-5 **$24.95**

Woman Spirit Awakening in Nature: Growing Into the Fullness of Who You Are
By Nancy Barrett Chickerneo, PhD; Foreword by Eileen Fisher
8 x 8, 224 pp, b/w illus., Quality PB, 978-1-59473-250-8 **$16.99**

Women of Color Pray: Voices of Strength, Faith, Healing, Hope and Courage
Edited and with Introductions by Christal M. Jackson
5 x 7¼, 208 pp, Quality PB, 978-1-59473-077-1 **$15.99**

* A book from Jewish Lights, SkyLight Paths' sister imprint

Prayer / Meditation

Men Pray: Voices of Strength, Faith, Healing, Hope and Courage
Created by the Editors at SkyLight Paths
Celebrates the rich variety of ways men around the world have called out to the Divine—with words of joy, praise, gratitude, wonder, petition and even anger—from the ancient world up to our own day.
5 x 7¼, 192 pp, HC, 978-1-59473-395-6 **$16.99**

Honest to God Prayer: Spirituality as Awareness, Empowerment, Relinquishment and Paradox
By Kent Ira Groff
For those turned off by shopworn religious language, offers innovative ways to pray based on both Native American traditions and Ignatian spirituality.
6 x 9, 192 pp, Quality PB, 978-1-59473-433-5 **$16.99**

Sacred Attention: A Spiritual Practice for Finding God in the Moment
By Margaret D. McGee
Framed on the Christian liturgical year, this inspiring guide explores ways to develop a practice of attention as a means of talking—and listening—to God.
6 x 9, 144 pp, Quality PB, 978-1-59473-291-1 **$16.99**

Women of Color Pray: Voices of Strength, Faith, Healing, Hope and Courage
Edited and with Introductions by Christal M. Jackson
Through these prayers, poetry, lyrics, meditations and affirmations, you will share in the strong and undeniable connection women of color share with God.
5 x 7¼, 208 pp, Quality PB, 978-1-59473-077-1 **$15.99**

Living into Hope: A Call to Spiritual Action for Such a Time as This
By Rev. Dr. Joan Brown Campbell; Foreword by Karen Armstrong
6 x 9, 208 pp, HC, 978-1-59473-283-6 **$21.99**

Praying with Our Hands: 21 Practices of Embodied Prayer from the World's Spiritual Traditions *By Jon M. Sweeney; Photos by Jennifer J. Wilson; Foreword by Mother Tessa Bielecki; Afterword by Taitetsu Unno, PhD*
8 x 8, 96 pp, 22 duotone photos, Quality PB, 978-1-893361-16-4 **$16.95**

Secrets of Prayer: A Multifaith Guide to Creating Personal Prayer in Your Life
By Nancy Corcoran, CSJ
6 x 9, 160 pp, Quality PB, 978-1-59473-215-7 **$16.99**

Three Gates to Meditation Practice: A Personal Journey into Sufism, Buddhism, and Judaism *By David A. Cooper* 5½ x 8½, 240 pp, Quality PB, 978-1-893361-22-5 **$16.95**

Prayer / M. Basil Pennington, OCSO

Finding Grace at the Center, 3rd Edition: The Beginning of Centering Prayer *With Thomas Keating, OCSO, and Thomas E. Clarke, SJ; Foreword by Rev. Cynthia Bourgeault, PhD* A practical guide to a simple and beautiful form of meditative prayer. 5 x 7¼,128 pp, Quality PB, 978-1-59473-182-2 **$12.99**

The Monks of Mount Athos: A Western Monk's Extraordinary Spiritual Journey on Eastern Holy Ground *Foreword by Archimandrite Dionysios*
Explores the landscape, monastic communities and food of Athos.
6 x 9, 352 pp, Quality PB, 978-1-893361-78-2 **$18.95**

Psalms: A Spiritual Commentary *Illus. by Phillip Ratner*
Reflections on some of the most beloved passages from the Bible's most widely read book. 6 x 9, 176 pp, 24 full-page b/w illus., Quality PB, 978-1-59473-234-8 **$16.99**

The Song of Songs: A Spiritual Commentary *Illus. by Phillip Ratner*
Explore the Bible's most challenging mystical text.
6 x 9, 160 pp, 14 full-page b/w illus., Quality PB, 978-1-59473-235-5 **$16.99**
HC, 978-1-59473-004-7 **$19.99**

Spiritual Poetry—The Mystic Poets

Experience these mystic poets as you never have before. Each beautiful, compact book includes a brief introduction to the poet's time and place, a summary of the major themes of the poet's mysticism and religious tradition, essential selections from the poet's most important works, and an appreciative preface by a contemporary spiritual writer.

Hafiz
The Mystic Poets
Translated and with Notes by Gertrude Bell
Preface by Ibrahim Gamard

Hafiz is known throughout the world as Persia's greatest poet, with sales of his poems in Iran today only surpassed by those of the Qur'an itself. His probing and joyful verse speaks to people from all backgrounds who long to taste and feel divine love and experience harmony with all living things.
5 x 7¼, 144 pp, HC, 978-1-59473-009-2 **$16.99**

Hopkins
The Mystic Poets
Preface by Rev. Thomas Ryan, CSP

Gerard Manley Hopkins, Christian mystical poet, is beloved for his use of fresh language and startling metaphors to describe the world around him. Although his verse is lovely, beneath the surface lies a searching soul, wrestling with and yearning for God.
5 x 7¼, 112 pp, HC, 978-1-59473-010-8 **$16.99**

Tagore
The Mystic Poets
Preface by Swami Adiswarananda

Rabindranath Tagore is often considered the Shakespeare of modern India. A great mystic, Tagore was the teacher of W. B. Yeats and Robert Frost, the close friend of Albert Einstein and Mahatma Gandhi, and the winner of the Nobel Prize for Literature. This beautiful sampling of Tagore's two most important works, *The Gardener* and *Gitanjali*, offers a glimpse into his spiritual vision that has inspired people around the world.
5 x 7¼, 144 pp, HC, 978-1-59473-008-5 **$16.99**

Whitman
The Mystic Poets
Preface by Gary David Comstock

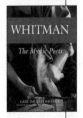

Walt Whitman was the most innovative and influential poet of the nineteenth century. This beautiful sampling of Whitman's most important poetry from *Leaves of Grass*, and selections from his prose writings, offers a glimpse into the spiritual side of his most radical themes—love for country, love for others and love of self.
5 x 7¼, 192 pp, HC, 978-1-59473-041-2 **$16.99**

Spiritual Practice

Fly-Fishing—The Sacred Art: Casting a Fly as a Spiritual Practice
By Rabbi Eric Eisenkramer and Rev. Michael Attas, MD; Foreword by Chris Wood, CEO,
Trout Unlimited; Preface by Lori Simon, executive director, Casting for Recovery
Shares what fly-fishing can teach you about reflection, awe and wonder; the benefits of solitude; the blessing of community and the search for the Divine.
5½ x 8½, 160 pp, Quality PB, 978-1-59473-299-7 **$16.99**

Lectio Divina—The Sacred Art: Transforming Words & Images into
Heart-Centered Prayer *By Christine Valters Paintner, PhD*
Expands the practice of sacred reading beyond scriptural texts and makes it
accessible in contemporary life. 5½ x 8½, 240 pp, Quality PB, 978-1-59473-300-0 **$16.99**

Writing—The Sacred Art: Beyond the Page to Spiritual Practice
By Rami Shapiro and Aaron Shapiro
Push your writing through the trite and the boring to something fresh, something
transformative. Includes over fifty unique, practical exercises.
5½ x 8½, 192 pp, Quality PB, 978-1-59473-372-7 **$16.99**

Conversation—The Sacred Art: Practicing Presence in an Age of Distraction
By Diane M. Millis, PhD; Foreword by Rev. Tilden Edwards, PhD
Cultivate the potential for deeper connection in every conversation.
5½ x 8½, 192 pp, Quality PB, 978-1-59473-474-8 **$16.99**

Pilgrimage—The Sacred Art: Journey to the Center of the Heart
By Dr. Sheryl A. Kujawa-Holbrook
Explore the many dimensions of the experience of pilgrimage—the yearning heart,
the painful setbacks, the encounter with the Divine and, ultimately, the changed
orientation to the world. 5½ x 8½, 240 pp, Quality PB, 978-1-59473-472-4 **$16.99**

Dance—The Sacred Art: The Joy of Movement as a Spiritual Practice
By Cynthia Winton-Henry 5½ x 8½, 224 pp, Quality PB, 978-1-59473-268-3 **$16.99**

Giving—The Sacred Art: Creating a Lifestyle of Generosity
By Lauren Tyler Wright 5½ x 8½, 208 pp, Quality PB, 978-1-59473-224-9 **$16.99**

Haiku—The Sacred Art: A Spiritual Practice in Three Lines
By Margaret D. McGee 5½ x 8½, 192 pp, Quality PB, 978-1-59473-269-0 **$16.99**

Hospitality—The Sacred Art: Discovering the Hidden Spiritual Power of Invitation
and Welcome *By Rev. Nanette Sawyer; Foreword by Rev. Dirk Ficca*
5½ x 8½, 208 pp, Quality PB, 978-1-59473-228-7 **$16.99**

Labyrinths from the Outside In, 2nd Edition: Walking to Spiritual Insight—A
Beginner's Guide *By Rev. Dr. Donna Schaper and Rev. Dr. Carole Ann Camp*
6 x 9, 208 pp, b/w illus. and photos, Quality PB, 978-1-59473-486-1 **$16.99**

Practicing the Sacred Art of Listening: A Guide to Enrich Your Relationships
and Kindle Your Spiritual Life *By Kay Lindahl* 8 x 8, 176 pp, Quality PB, 978-1-893361-85-0 **$16.95**

Recovery—The Sacred Art: The Twelve Steps as Spiritual Practice *by Rami Shapiro;*
Foreword by Joan Borysenko, PhD 5½ x 8½, 240 pp, Quality PB, 978-1-59473-259-1 **$16.99**

Running—The Sacred Art: Preparing to Practice *By Dr. Warren A. Kay; Foreword by*
Kristin Armstrong 5½ x 8½, 160 pp, Quality PB, 978-1-59473-227-0 **$16.99**

The Sacred Art of Chant: Preparing to Practice
By Ana Hernández 5½ x 8½, 192 pp, Quality PB, 978-1-59473-036-8 **$16.99**

The Sacred Art of Fasting: Preparing to Practice
By Thomas Ryan, CSP 5½ x 8½, 192 pp, Quality PB, 978-1-59473-078-8 **$15.99**

The Sacred Art of Forgiveness: Forgiving Ourselves and Others through God's Grace
By Marcia Ford 8 x 8, 176 pp, Quality PB, 978-1-59473-175-4 **$18.99**

The Sacred Art of Listening: Forty Reflections for Cultivating a Spiritual Practice
By Kay Lindahl; Illus. by Amy Schnapper 8 x 8, 160 pp, b/w illus., Quality PB, 978-1-893361-44-7 **$16.95**

The Sacred Art of Lovingkindness: Preparing to Practice
By Rabbi Rami Shapiro; Foreword by Marcia Ford 5¼ x 8¼, 176 pp, Quality PB, 978-1-59473-151-8 **$16.99**

Thanking & Blessing—The Sacred Art: Spiritual Vitality through Gratefulness
By Jay Marshall, PhD; Foreword by Philip Gulley 5½ x 8½, 176 pp, Quality PB, 978-1-59473-231-7 **$16.99**

Spirituality

The Passionate Jesus: What We Can Learn from Jesus about Love, Fear, Grief, Joy and Living Authentically
By The Rev. Peter Wallace
Reveals Jesus as a passionate figure who was involved, present, connected, honest and direct with others and encourages you to build personal authenticity in every area of your own life.
6 x 9, 208 pp, Quality PB, 978-1-59473-393-2 **$18.99**

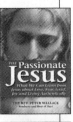

Gathering at God's Table: The Meaning of Mission in the Feast of Faith
By Katharine Jefferts Schori
A profound reminder of our role in the larger frame of God's dream for a restored and reconciled world. 6 x 9, 256 pp, HC, 978-1-59473-316-1 **$21.99**

The Heartbeat of God: Finding the Sacred in the Middle of Everything
By Katharine Jefferts Schori; Foreword by Joan Chittister, OSB
Explores our connections to other people, to other nations and with the environment through the lens of faith. 6 x 9, 240 pp, HC, 978-1-5947-3-292-8 **$21.99**

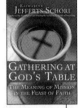

A Dangerous Dozen: Twelve Christians Who Threatened the Status Quo but Taught Us to Live Like Jesus
By the Rev. Canon C. K. Robertson, PhD; Foreword by Archbishop Desmond Tutu
Profiles twelve visionary men and women who challenged society and showed the world a different way of living. 6 x 9, 208 pp, Quality PB, 978-1-5947-3-298-0 **$16.99**

Decision Making & Spiritual Discernment: The Sacred Art of Finding Your Way *By Nancy L. Bieber*
Presents three essential aspects of Spirit-led decision making: willingness, attentiveness and responsiveness. 5½ x 8½, 208 pp, Quality PB, 978-1-5947-3-289-8 **$16.99**

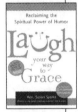

Laugh Your Way to Grace: Reclaiming the Spiritual Power of Humor
By Rev. Susan Sparks A powerful, humorous case for laughter as a spiritual, healing path. 6 x 9, 176 pp, Quality PB, 978-1-5947-3-280-5 **$16.99**

Bread, Body, Spirit: Finding the Sacred in Food
Edited and with Introductions by Alice Peck 6 x 9, 224 pp, Quality PB, 978-1-5947-3-242-3 **$19.99**

Claiming Earth as Common Ground: The Ecological Crisis through the Lens of Faith
By Andrea Cohen-Kiener; Foreword by Rev. Sally Bingham
6 x 9, 192 pp, Quality PB, 978-1-5947-3-261-4 **$16.99**

Creating a Spiritual Retirement: A Guide to the Unseen Possibilities in Our Lives
By Molly Srode 6 x 9, 208 pp, b/w photos, Quality PB, 978-1-5947-3-050-4 **$14.99**

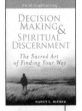

Creative Aging: Rethinking Retirement and Non-Retirement in a Changing World
By Marjory Zoet Bankson 6 x 9, 160 pp, Quality PB, 978-1-5947-3-281-2 **$16.99**

Keeping Spiritual Balance as We Grow Older: More than 65 Creative Ways to Use Purpose, Prayer, and the Power of Spirit to Build a Meaningful Retirement
By Molly and Bernie Srode 8 x 8, 224 pp, Quality PB, 978-1-5947-3-042-9 **$16.99**

Hearing the Call across Traditions: Readings on Faith and Service
Edited by Adam Davis; Foreword by Eboo Patel 6 x 9, 352 pp, Quality PB, 978-1-5947-3-303-1 **$18.99**

Honoring Motherhood: Prayers, Ceremonies & Blessings
Edited and with Introductions by Lynn L. Caruso
5 x 7¼, 272 pp, Quality PB, 978-1-58473-384-0 **$9.99**; HC, 978-1-5947-3-239-3 **$19.99**

The Losses of Our Lives: The Sacred Gifts of Renewal in Everyday Loss
By Dr. Nancy Copeland-Payton 6 x 9, 192 pp, HC, 978-1-5947-3-271-3 **$19.99**

Renewal in the Wilderness: A Spiritual Guide to Connecting with God in the Natural World *By John Lionberger* 6 x 9, 176 pp, b/w photos, Quality PB, 978-1-5947-3-219-5 **$16.99**

Soul Fire: Accessing Your Creativity
By Thomas Ryan, CSP 6 x 9, 160 pp, Quality PB, 978-1-5947-3-243-0 **$16.99**

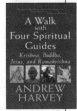

A Spirituality for Brokenness: Discovering Your Deepest Self in Difficult Times
By Terry Taylor 6 x 9, 176 pp, Quality PB, 978-1-5947-3-229-4 **$16.99**

A Walk with Four Spiritual Guides: Krishna, Buddha, Jesus, and Ramakrishna
By Andrew Harvey 5½ x 8½, 192 pp, b/w photos & illus., Quality PB, 978-1-5947-3-138-9 **$15.99**

About SKYLIGHT PATHS Publishing

SkyLight Paths Publishing is creating a place where people of different spiritual traditions come together for challenge and inspiration, a place where we can help each other understand the mystery that lies at the heart of our existence.

Through spirituality, our religious beliefs are increasingly becoming a part of our lives—rather than *apart* from our lives. While many of us may be more interested than ever in spiritual growth, we may be less firmly planted in traditional religion. Yet, we do want to deepen our relationship to the sacred, to learn from our own as well as from other faith traditions, and to practice in new ways.

SkyLight Paths sees both believers and seekers as a community that increasingly transcends traditional boundaries of religion and denomination—people wanting to learn from each other, *walking together, finding the way.*

For your information and convenience, at the back of this book we have provided a list of other SkyLight Paths books you might find interesting and useful. They cover the following subjects:

Buddhism / Zen	Global Spiritual	Monasticism
Catholicism	Perspectives	Mysticism
Children's Books	Gnosticism	Poetry
Christianity	Hinduism /	Prayer
Comparative	Vedanta	Religious Etiquette
Religion	Inspiration	Retirement
Current Events	Islam / Sufism	Spiritual Biography
Earth-Based	Judaism	Spiritual Direction
Spirituality	Kabbalah	Spirituality
Enneagram	Meditation	Women's Interest
	Midrash Fiction	Worship

Or phone, fax, mail or e-mail to: SKYLIGHT PATHS Publishing
Sunset Farm Offices, Route 4 • P.O. Box 237 • Woodstock, Vermont 05091
Tel: (802) 457-4000 • Fax: (802) 457-4004 • www.skylightpaths.com
Credit card orders: (800) 962-4544 (8:30AM–5:30PM EST Monday–Friday)
Generous discounts on quantity orders. SATISFACTION GUARANTEED. Prices subject to change.